Walk Through Fire

Walk Through Fire

To Molly

One Couple's Journey of Findiing Joy in the Midst of Tragedy

Always Choose Joy!

Carly Bowers

Carly and David Bowers

with A.J. Gregory

Fedd Books
P.O. Box 341973
Austin, TX 78734
www.thefeddagency.com

Published in association with the The Fedd Agency, Inc., a literary agency.

Scripture quotations marked NLT are taken from the *Holy Bible*, New Living Translation, copyright ©1996, 2004, 2007, 2013 by Tyndale House Foundation. Used by permission of Tyndale House Publishers, Inc., Carol Stream, Illinois 60188. All rights reserved.

Scripture quotations marked NIV are taken from the Holy Bible, New International Version ®, NIV ®. Copyright © 1973, 1978, 1984, 2011 by Biblica, Inc. ® Used by permission of Zondervan. All rights reserved worldwide. www.zondervan.com.

Tim Robbins, *The Shawshank Redemption*, directed by Frank Darabont, (1994; Castle Rock Entertainment, 2008), DVD.

Spirit Song, written and composed by John Wimber. Copyright: © 1979 MERCY/VINEYARD PUBLISHING (ASCAP) ADMIN. IN NORTH AMERICA BY MUSIC SERVICES o/b/o VINEYARD MUSIC USA. Used by permission.

ISBN: 978-1-943217-10-6
eISBN: 978-1-943217-11-3

Library of Congress Control Number: 2015950702
Cover and Interior Design by Lauren Hall
Cover Photograph by Amber Hecko
Editorial development by AJ Gregory

Printed in the United States of America
First Edition 15 14 13 10 09 / 10 9 8 7 6 5 4 3 2 1

To our amazing God, who continues to do immeasurably more than we could ever imagine and who is always faithful.

To our children, Samantha & Nathan, we love you for who you have become, in spite of the hardships you've had to overcome.

And to you, the reader, we pray that by sharing our story, you might find encouragement to walk through whatever life throws at you.

1.

Carly

A ringing phone during a baby's nap is an unwelcome interruption. Most mothers will tell you this. Their nap equals time for you, and usually involves mundane tasks like catching up on laundry, cleaning up the lunch mess, or if you're lucky, taking a well-deserved breather. So God help—and I mean that—whatever or whoever barges in on that precious time and wakes a sleeping child.

On August 20, 1999, the day life divided quickly and without warning into before and after, my two-year-old son, Nathan, slept soundly during his nap. I sat at the desk in my home office and scribbled notes, tweaking my lesson plan for an upcoming youth meeting at my church.

Enter the ringing phone.

I won't lie. I was annoyed, ready to chew off the ear of the telemarketer I was pretty confident was at the other end.

"Hello," I said, not even trying to fake chipper.

"Is this Carly Bowers?" a woman on the other line asked.

"Yes, can I help you?"

I would have never been prepared for what came next, nor will I ever forget those life-changing words.

"My name is so-and-so. I'm a nurse at St. Mary's Hospital over in Port Arthur. Your husband David has been in an accident, a serious explosion at work. You need to come down to the emergency room as soon as possible."

I heard the words, or at least part of me did. The other part started slipping away, detaching from my body as if floating on a cloud. One part living and breathing; the other motionless, numbed by disbelief.

The dial tone sounded on the other end of the receiver as the room started to spin in nauseating circles. *Husband. Accident. Explosion. Come now.* The words repeated in my brain, disorienting my thinking.

I knew I had to get to the hospital, now. I also knew I had a sleeping toddler just down the hall and an eight-year-old daughter, Samantha, in the middle of her school day working out fractions or learning about the solar system. So how then? How was I going to get to the hospital when I couldn't even figure out the next step of what to do with my children?

In the middle of trying to process logistics while unanswerable questions churned in my head about my husband's condition, a miracle. The doorbell rang. As I numbly turned the knob, outside the house stood David's manager, Clyde Howard, a tall man with gray hair and a serious but kind face, and his gracious wife, Linda, a local schoolteacher with a beautiful smile and wavy auburn hair.

"Carly," they said almost in unison, their faces white as ghosts. A sickening feeling came over me.

They knew.

They knew what had happened to David.

Clyde was a rock. He's always been that way. David loved being under his leadership at the Praxair plant in Groves, Texas. Though Clyde was the higher-up, he never acted like it. He treated the men he served with dignity and respect. And it was never beneath him to do a subordinate job that wasn't his responsibility simply because it had to get done. Clyde took care of his men, often inviting them and their families over for dinner, and always keeping an open door policy of communication. Dave and I had spent a lot of time with Clyde and Linda socially, and enjoyed each other's company.

"We are so sorry," Linda said sympathetically, her eyes welling with tears.

My questions tumbled out with force. "How's Dave? Do you know what happened? Is he going to be okay? How badly is he hurt?"

I don't remember Clyde offering much more information than the nurse had given me. I do know he was upset because he had wanted me to hear the news from him, in person, not some stranger over the telephone. Linda offered to stay and wake up Nathan, pick Samantha up at school, and meet us afterwards at the hospital.

Linda looked worried, asking, "What do I tell Sam?"

Good question. "Just the basics," I replied, not entirely confident in parental protocol at this point. "Just say that her dad was in an accident." Then again, there wasn't much to say. None of us knew more than that.

Linda nodded as I rummaged through the kitchen, trying to remember where I had left my purse. I struggled with not having a plan or a strategy, some form of defense against the unknown. Seems silly, right? You can't really prepare for what you don't know.

Quiet, Clyde drove the twenty minutes from where we lived in Nederland, Texas to St. Mary's. I stared out the passenger window, signs of the perfect suburban life blurring into an unrecognizable fog of live oak trees, trimmed shrubbery, and identical houses with driveways littered by toppled children's bicycles.

I prayed. Nothing long and drawn out. I prayed the only word that I hoped would bring me peace, clarity, comfort. The only word I knew that could—Jesus.

Jesus.

Jesus.

Oh, sweet Jesus.

Clyde handed me his cell phone so I could call my parents, Chuck and Rosemary, David's parents, Keith and Marilyn, and the church where we served. It was the strangest thing. No one answered. I clicked the "off" button right when we pulled into the Emergency Room entrance, a destination swarming with flashing lights and sirens from incoming traumas.

Clyde led me past the waiting room and down a short hallway. An open door or two offered glimpses of doctors dispensing orders and procedure instructions, nurses rushing around tending to patients surrounded by batteries of beeping machines and webs of tubes and wires. Though we weren't sure which room he was in, it didn't take long for us to find David. I smelled him even before I could see him. The rancid odor was distinctive, penetrating my nostrils with the unmistakable stench of charred flesh. It's a smell you never forget.

While Clyde stayed put in the hallway, I walked into the doorway of the bustling room cranked to high speed. My stomach churned. My husband. There he was, lying naked on a table, burned to a crisp on what looked like every inch of his body. A layer of crackled black covered his raw, red, and bleeding flesh. As a team of doctors and nurses furiously worked to monitor his breathing and manage his pain, someone in scrubs stood in the corner on the phone, figuring out the nearest burn center that had an available bed. This hospital wasn't equipped to treat the full extent of David's injuries.

"I'm his wife," I blurted out, talking to no one in particular, my voice trembling.

"You have a minute or two before we need to intubate," a doctor stated with a grim expression on her face. "And then we need to get him out of here."

By how badly burned David looked, I was surprised he was even conscious as I gathered up whatever little strength I had to say goodbye. My chest tightened as I thought of that word—goodbye. What did it mean? Goodbye forever? Goodbye until we get to the burn unit? Was this it?

I stood over the table where my husband lay, his face akin to a butchered slab of meat. In the movies, these moments are usually long and drawn out, filled with long-winded sappy speeches where you articulate, quite poetically, exactly what you want to say. The reality was anything but.

"I love you, honey," I whispered, putting my face as close

to his as possible. I couldn't touch him because of how badly he was hurt.

David managed a weak smile, his breath labored and heavy. "I love you, too, Carly. Don't worry, everything is going to be okay." Maybe it sounds selfish, but in that moment I needed, oh so desperately, to hear that. David's words were reassuring, especially because he said it with a smile.

But then came the contradiction.

"Take care of the kids, Carly."

And with that, my heart fell.

Our interaction couldn't have lasted more than a minute before I was ushered out of the room so the medical team could sedate him and get him ready for helicopter transport.

Take care of the kids.

Those weren't words of comfort. It's usually what you say before something bad happens. *Was David going to die?* It was the only conclusion I could come to. The words weighing heavily, I could barely remember his assurance that everything was going to be okay, let alone his consistent smile. Clyde stood by me as we waited in stunned silence in a hallway, stark and cold, for more information when the doctor who had been treating David came over to me.

"I'm sorry to say this, Mrs. Bowers, but you need to be prepared. Your husband's injuries have a high mortality rate." My heart, my hope, fell even further. *Mortality. Death.* I began to panic. I wasn't ready to say goodbye to David. I wasn't ready to be a widow at twenty-six.

From the corner of my eye I could see a nurses' station nearby, women in pale blue scrubs thumbing quickly through medical charts and making phone calls in hushed tones. I crumbled to the floor in shock. I felt like I was going to vomit. And I did, in a nearby trashcan. Clyde helped me as I stumbled over to the waiting room, where I sat for the next few minutes staring blindly at crisp white walls covered in cheap artwork.

More people started filling up the waiting area, some folks I knew from church, David's work, others who weren't familiar. A nurse I hadn't seen before came in at some point. With compassionate eyes, she knelt beside me and asked, "Carly, can you come with me?" I nodded. This gracious lady led me to a small private area, quiet.

"Are you a praying woman?" she asked.

I nodded.

"Then, I'd like to pray with you," the nurse said, clasping my hands in hers. So together, as tears stung my cheeks, we asked God for mercy, for comfort. And above all, in faith, we thanked Him for overcoming and conquering death—because that's what we both knew David was facing. Death. I'll never forget this woman, the first out of an endless stream of people, loved ones and strangers alike, who offered prayers, sympathies, and encouragement. I will always be grateful for every single one of them.

As arrangements were finalized to life-flight David to the Blocker Burn Unit at UTMB (University of Texas Medical Branch) in Galveston, two and a half hours away, I remained planted on the vinyl seats in the waiting room, Clyde by my side as well as Gaylene Holt, the wife of David's co-worker, Mark, who worked across the street from the hospital. Mark had called her after David was rushed off the plant property via ambulance and asked her to sit with me in the emergency room. Not only did Gaylene pray with me, but after arming her with a list of phone numbers, she helped make phone calls to family members and friends who lived out of town and wouldn't have heard the news via word of mouth. The waiting room filled up by the minute, as those who had heard of the accident and were nearby came to offer support. As I stared at the faces of our friends, I was overwhelmed by the outpouring of love.

Though it seemed time was passing excruciatingly slowly, it had only been less than an hour since I arrived at the hospital. And not long after, Linda showed up with Samantha and Nathan. My little guy was too young to understand the chaotic level of panic, but worry was written all over Samantha's face.

She rushed toward me, and asked, her voice cracking, "How's Daddy? Is he going to be okay?"

I brushed my daughter's silky brown hair away from her forehead, wanting to say something, anything, so I could trade the fear, the worry, in her eyes with her characteristic carefree cheer. But I couldn't. I couldn't pretend. I had no choice but to give an honest answer. Yes, as a parent, it's our job to protect our kids. It's our responsibility to keep them safe, to shield them from what could possibly hurt them. But in this case, staring into my daughter's face, the fact was that just down the hall her father was fighting for his life, covered head to toe in burned skin with God only knew how much damage to his lungs from smoke inhalation. So no, I couldn't force a happy face and glibly brush off the obvious, as ugly and heartbreaking as it was.

I held Samantha closely, running my fingers through her hair. "I don't know, honey. Daddy was hurt pretty bad. But we're going to pray that no matter what happens, we're going to be okay."

She nodded, asking more questions and me answering them with a simple statement. "All we can do is pray and trust God." As my daughter rested in my arms, the room stood still. All of the background noise—the apprehensive chatter, the whispered prayers, the nervous taps of feet—dulled. I closed my eyes, inhaling the scent of my little girl's hair, and sighed.

Jesus. Oh, Jesus.

David

I was scheduled to be off that day. And boy did I need it! I had been putting in a ridiculous amount of hours at work as an assistant plant manager for Praxair, one of the largest industrial gas companies worldwide. Several months earlier, Praxair had been contracted to build a new plant inside the facility in order to supply additional product to our customer. The work was demanding, requiring long hours and being on call 24/7. After long weeks of brainstorming and implementing and a few unsuccessful starts, the new plant was finally functioning. We were only days away from making product and putting it down the pipeline. Clyde, both boss and good friend, whom I had worked with previously at a plant in East Chicago, and I headed up the team as management at the plant in Groves, Texas. He worked twelve-hour shifts during the day and I did the same but at night during this start up phase.

I went to work as scheduled on Thursday, August 19, 1999 at 6 p.m. when Clyde greeted me with a wide smile and a slap on the back. "Go home, Dave," he said. "And

take Friday off. There's nothing left to do. We're all set."
His words were music to my ears but I didn't immediately
take off. Instead, I tinkered around with a few things until I
finally left at midnight.

For the first time in a long time, I was able to sleep next
to my wife. As the sun made its way up over the horizon, we
enjoyed a lover's moment, the last normal we would ever
have together.

When I woke Samantha up for school that morning, her
eyes burst wide open and she beamed. "Daddy! Daddy!
You're here!" When I told her I was going to have breakfast
with her at school, well, she just about shot up out of bed
and got ready in ten seconds flat. Chitchatting with some of
the other parents on the cafeteria line, I noticed what Sam
had piled on to her plastic yellow tray.

"Chocolate milk? You sure you want to put chocolate
milk on those Frosted Flakes, Sam?"

My daughter just grinned, baring her teeth through a
sugary sweet smile. Our visit was short but sweet. "I love
you, Samantha," I said when it was time to say goodbye,
planting a kiss on her cheek.

As I drove the short ride home from my daughter's school,
I thought about the agenda for the day. The way the startup
was progressing, I knew a move to another Praxair facility
was inevitable. Once the new plant was up and running, the
plan was for the family and me to relocate out of Texas to
East Chicago, where a position had just opened up. Though
the news was relatively fresh, things happened pretty fast
at Praxair. Knowing this, Carly and I had recently met with
a realtor in town to sell our home. So on my unexpected day
off, my wife and I blocked out time to figure out logistics.

No offense against the Lone Star State, but we were anxious to move closer to the Midwest, where our family was scattered.

I didn't stay long at the house. Knowing the rest of the team was at the plant, I started feeling anxious. Despite what Clyde had said, I knew there was always something to be done. And there was no way I was going to take the whole day off while everyone else was plugging away at finalizing the startup process. So by mid-morning, I headed back to the plant.

After working on a few things and enjoying a mouth-watering lunch at a local Mexican joint that made the world's best quesadillas right at your table, it came to my attention that we had a faulty flow meter, a mechanism that is used to measure how much product courses through a particular pipeline. It was one of the last items on our checklist of things to do before the new plant was considered a success and ready to run.

Clyde, a handful of other engineers, and I crowded the control room and analyzed ideas on how to get it done. It wasn't a task that had standard protocol. You had to first isolate that section of piping, remove the pressure from it, and then could replace the flow meter and put it in service. Sounds simple, right? Well, in some ways, Clyde and I thought so.

At around 1:30 p.m., the two of us took a walk outside through the maze of piping, giant air compressors, chillers, purifiers, and cooling towers. When we arrived at the problem location, Clyde and I closed a few valves to isolate the piping. I hopped on a six-foot ladder and tried to open one particular two-inch valve that would allow us to vent the pressure through the pipe, but the darn thing was stuck. As hard as I tried, I could not for the life of me pry it open. I stood on top of that metal ladder, sweltering in the Texas heat, feeling every degree of 90, blanketed with 100% humidity. There was no need to exert unnecessary energy to find a tool to open the valve so I called below to Clyde.

"Hey, get me a pipe wrench, will you? I can't get this thing open."

"Sure thing," he called out over his shoulder, starting to make his way to the maintenance shop.

As sweat dripped down every inch of my body, my eyes were drawn to a cluster of sparks on the side of the pipe. I couldn't hear anything, but instinct and experience told me the piping was catching on fire. And it doesn't take a genius to understand that sparks around an oxygen pipeline does not a happy ending make. I had to get out of there—and fast.

Immediately, I leapt off the ladder, making a conscious and intuitive decision to hold my breath. I remembered a story my father told me when I was a little boy where a friend of his opened a bedroom door during a house fire. As he gasped at the sight of the fire, the flames burned his lungs and he was killed.

I jumped off the ladder and took a step or two away from it, when the pipe released a burst of pressure, immediately flooding the place with oxygen. While oxygen isn't flammable and by itself doesn't burn, it will ignite any flammable object or substance in its path. And that's exactly what happened.

I didn't hear any noise, no warning. Only a blinding, explosive flash as I began to roll on the gravel-covered ground, engulfed in violent flames. The intense pain I felt was unbearable at first, but as seconds and minutes passed, the pain lessened. It felt like a relief at the time, but it was only because, unbeknownst to me, I was covered in third-degree burns, many of my nerves were damaged, consumed by the fire.

Shell-shocked, I had no idea if the fire was still raging, if I was still being licked raw by the flames. Having held my breath for so long, I couldn't do it anymore. I exhaled, gasping for air. Managing to pull myself together, still in a considerable amount of pain, I sat up in the gravel. I felt hot. Wait, that's an understatement. I felt scalded, which, of course, I was. Later, an expert would estimate that the temperatures of the flash fire that had consumed me skyrocketed as high as 3,000-5,000 degrees for a few seconds.

I seethed, my feet and my armpits swelling with hot pain. Anger coursed through my veins. Though I couldn't fully comprehend the extent of my injuries, I was mad I got hurt in what I considered to be a safe place to work. Oh sure, there were risks. There always are. But I was a safety precaution zealot. As was Clyde. We meticulously followed every protocol, every procedure, and every rule in the book to prevent injuries and accidents. And our track record thus far was impeccable. No one had ever gotten hurt on our watch. But here I was, sitting in the hot Texas sun, gravel digging into my burned skin.

This is crazy. I can't believe this happened, I ranted, using a string of much more colorful words.

My daughter's ninth birthday was three days away and I was angry that I probably wouldn't be able to enjoy her pool party. Knowing I'd been burned, I assumed I wouldn't be physically able to swim and play games with her in the community pool for at least a few days. Maybe I'd even need to stay in the hospital for that long.

"I can't believe this," I roared, continuing to cuss like a sailor. The rage intensified as I discovered more things to be mad about. I was angry I was alone. No one had come for me.

Where on earth was everyone? Surely, someone knows something happened. Why isn't anybody here?

I didn't realize in the moment, but it had been less than a minute since the flash fire. I'd find out later that some folks on our team were hiding in the control room, fearing the entire plant was going to explode and others were trying to figure out what had happened.

It was time to take matters into my own hands. I picked myself off the ground, much of my energy fueled by my growing rage, and staggered my way over to the control room. I wasn't but a few feet away when I saw the outline of a person. It was Paul, a co-worker. I couldn't quite make out what he was doing, but it looked like he was heading the other way, away from me.

"Where are you going?" I called out. Heck, maybe it wasn't him. Maybe I was delirious, seeing a ghost.

My eyeglasses were nowhere to be found and since my eyesight was so bad, I couldn't tell how badly my body was burned. By then I could see that I was naked, wearing only high-top leather boots and a leather belt. Upon impact, the fiery blast had disintegrated every other article of clothing. My feet felt like they were still on fire and I wanted nothing more than to get those blasted leather boots off. But no matter how hard I pulled or tugged at the shoestrings, they wouldn't budge.

A panicked and pale Paul came back, carrying a cooler of water. He dumped the five-gallon container over me, the rush of the liquid releasing steam from my body. I turned to Paul and said, "Get me more water!" My voice was strained with a hint of impatience. "And I think I might need an ambulance, too!" Paul sped off.

"Good God, my feet hurt," I moaned, once again trying to yank my boots off, eventually kicking one off my foot and ripping off the sole of the boot in the process. I noticed I couldn't get my fingers and hands to work. The harder I tried to pull at the other boot, the more I felt like all thumbs. As I drew my hands up to my face, I realized my skin was falling off.

This is bad. Real bad. It was starting to click, though ever so slowly, that I was likely in a lot worse shape than I had first thought.

My body felt like it was on fire. I needed to cool the burns and I couldn't wait around, helpless, for Paul to get back. I decided to forge ahead and staggered back up and over to a nearby cooling tower, a couple hundred feet away. The water wasn't clean or very cool, mind you, roasting at around 95 degrees, but still, water was water. I awkwardly shoved my head under a spout I was easily able to knock open, sighing in relief as the liquid soothed the burns. I couldn't figure out how to get the rest of my body under the running water, but at least I felt a little better.

As I wobbled towards the control room, I saw Mark Holt, my co-worker and good friend, coming around a corner of pipeline. Even though my vision wasn't great, I could still see the look on his face. Fear and dread washed over him as all color drained from his skin. The first words that came out of his mouth were a prayer. Something like, "Please Jesus, please be with Dave." We stared at each other in silence while Mark repeated that simple plea over and over and over.

My engineering mind tried to compose the scattered pieces of what had happened into a clearer picture. My injuries had to be bad, probably life-threatening. It was a wonder I could still walk, though when you're running on pure adrenaline, anything is possible. Listening to Mark pray gave me pause. It made me rethink the barrage of anger that overwhelmed me. In that moment, I surrendered and refocused my attention on my Heavenly Father instead of the still foggy picture of my situation and my growing anger.

"God, it is well with my soul. If it's my time to go, I'm okay with that. I don't want to, but if that's the plan, then so be it. But, Lord, if I can stay here and take care of my family, well, I'd really like that." I had no desire to use my circumstance as a bargaining chip. I wasn't going to beg God to spare me and in return promise to spend the rest of my life as a missionary in some third world country. I submitted, humbly, to what He deemed best. He was in control, after all, and I'd trusted Him practically my whole life. So why stop now?

After my mind settled, I whispered to Mark, "Cut my boots off."

Paul returned with another cooler full of water, poured it over, me and splashed some water onto my armpits. Still praying, Mark dropped to his knees, whipped out a Leatherman tool and cut off my boots. I let out a sigh as he, as gently as he possibly could, propped me up against the side of his body and together we made our way over to the control room, slow and steady.

Knowing I was naked and remembering we had two female co-workers who would be in the control room, I asked Mark for a blanket, which he got right away as we entered the doorway.

Without my glasses, I still couldn't see very well. But I made out similar looks of horror, dread on all who occupied the control room. And I definitely heard the whispers of concern. Everyone was worried but tried not to let it show that much. It didn't matter. I already knew I was hurt badly. I sat on an uncomfortable chair in the control room, swaddled in a blanket.

I closed my eyes while waiting for the ambulance and fire department to arrive. Time passed slowly, as it always does when you're waiting. All I could do was keep praying. Frankly, it wasn't just my only option, it was the best one. It was during those last few moments at that plant, the transition from anger to surrender, that peace became a companion. Resting in me, washing over me. This kind of peace isn't a human one. It's not something we can manufacture on our own. It's inexplicable. The against-all-odds kind. It's a peace that can only come from Christ.

Suddenly, I heard the wail of sirens, louder and louder, and then the sprinting of the firemen's rubber-soled shoes rushing through the control room toward me. Clothed in heavily insulated suits, one of the guys placed a cold burn dressing on my face just as the pain really started to set in. I wasn't running on adrenaline anymore. The shock was wearing off, and fast. Paramedics rushed in just seconds later.

"How are we going to get him out of the chair?" one of the first responders asked another in a whisper that was much too loud. I looked down at my body, raw skin peering through the unblanketed areas. There wasn't any touchable skin left to grab hold of to move me elsewhere.

"I'll do it myself," I offered. "I'll get up and walk to the stretcher."

"You can do that?" one of the paramedics asked, unconvinced. Nobody seemed enthused by my suggestion, but there wasn't an alternative.

I nodded. "Yeah, pretty sure I can."

It took every ounce of will and strength to pitch my body over to the stretcher as I seared with pain. My breathing heavy, an EMT helped me lay back and gave me oxygen. And then, in a blur of rush and frenzy, I was wheeled into an ambulance, sirens bellowing and lights flashing, heading toward the nearest hospital, St. Mary's.

"Hi David, I'm Jay. Are you married?" asked one of the paramedics who sat beside me in the ambulance, shooting me with hits of morphine and monitoring my oxygen. I didn't know it at the time, but Jay had administered the entire supply of morphine the ambulance stocked during the short ride to the ER.

Faint and weak, I nodded. "Yeah."

"Any kids?"

"Two," I mumbled. I was fading, being pummeled by intense waves of pain and crushing exhaustion. The sounds of the sirens were barely audible as my level of consciousness started dropping. All I wanted to do was close my eyes. And sleep.

Then, he started asking me questions about hobbies,

whether or not I liked to fish. The chatter wasn't baseless. As a paramedic, he knew talking would ensure an open airway and therefore, the fact that I was breathing.

I didn't feel like exchanging chitchat about bass or tackle or poles. I didn't want to talk at all, for that matter. But if talking was the activity du jour, then I wanted to talk answers. I couldn't piece together the extent of my injuries on horrified looks alone. I needed some sort of confirmation from a medical professional.

"How bad is it?" I asked Jay.

His face somber, he pulled no punches. "Pretty bad."

It wasn't that I didn't think my injuries were severe, but I needed to hear it from someone else, not just my instincts. And believe it or not his two words prepared me, however little, for the fight I knew was coming.

By the time I was wheeled into the emergency room and swarmed by doctors and nurses, my muscles started to contract and forced my body to curl up into a fetal position. My chest tightening, I could barely breathe as I listened to more medical personnel hammering me with questions.

"What's your wife's name?"

I remember giving someone the phone numbers to our home, our church and our dear friend, Jackie Philyaw. They were trying to get a hold of Carly. In between heaving gasps, I tried my best to answer whatever was being asked. The morphine kept coming as did barked orders from doctors for this and that. One doctor mentioned she had to intubate me but wanted to wait because my wife was on her way.

Barely able to muster a whisper above clamor I asked her, "So what's my situation?"

"I'm sorry, sir. You have a high mortality injury. Chances

of survival are slim to none."

I didn't like those odds. "Well, alright," I told the doctor. "Then get busy because it's not my time yet." The last thing I remember was talking to Carly, telling her I loved her and that everything was going to be okay.

And then, I finally went to sleep.

Carly

A gowned nurse rushed into the now standing room-only waiting room. "Carly?" And when our eyes met, "Please come with me, your husband is ready for transport."

Samantha and Nathan stayed in the waiting room while Clyde accompanied me to the top floor of the hospital. When the elevator lurched to a stop, my nerves got the best of me. Shaking, I tried to be strong, leaning somewhat on Clyde's arm as we followed the nurse down a short hallway. I knew I had to buck up. Pull my chin up and face whatever was coming head-on. I didn't want to. I certainly didn't know how. But I needed to. When the nurse pushed open a large metal door that opened to the roof, gusts of wind slapped our faces. The shiny orange aircraft was only a few yards away, resting loudly on a helipad.

And then paramedics, maybe even a doctor or two, hustled toward the helicopter, clutching the sides of the rolling stretcher on which David lay. The roar of the aircraft sounded louder as I made my way toward my husband. I couldn't stay long as the space was especially cramped, but I whispered a final "I love you," to my now sedated husband, covered in bandages, blankets, and IVs hanging out of his arm. Then, the pilot signaled it was time for takeoff and I rushed back to the roof entrance. As the doors of the helicopter closed and blades spun furiously, it was all I could do to hang on to Clyde and not collapse.

Was this it?

Will I ever see my husband alive again?

I watched the aircraft glide up and away from the roof, my short hair spinning in every direction. My eyes fixed on the helicopter until it became an undistinguishable speck on the horizon. Facing the unknown was paralyzing. I heard someone define despair as the absence of any positive expectation. I felt that. In light of how bad David's burns were, in light of the doctor's grim report to extinguish optimistic expectations, and in light of my husband's final words to me to take care of our kids, hope had been spent.

I stayed on the roof for what seemed like a long time. On the outside, I was stoic, staring into space paralyzed by the preceding events. On the inside, memories flooded my mind like a movie reel, snapshots of David and me meeting for the first time, our wedding day, family vacations frolicking in sand and surf with our kids. I wondered if this was where the reel was supposed to end.

2.

Carly

As a kid I remember being angry at God a lot. Mainly, at first, because of what my father had gone through. When he was in his early 30s, my dad, Chuck, was crushed by a Coca-Cola machine at work. He was permanently disabled by the accident. Though he could walk, he was in a lot of pain and would never be able to work again. Dad was home a lot and so through a series of impromptu conversations, I learned about his background. How when he was five, he lost his father in a drowning accident; how two years later, his sister Myrla was killed in a car accident; how his mom died when he was thirteen and afterwards he bounced around in foster homes. My heart hurt for my father, who was a caring and funny man, always inserting just enough humor into life to keep from taking it too seriously.

Though church wasn't a part of our life, I still believed a Divine Being existed. I just thought he was a lousy God. And I blamed Him not just for the terrible chain of events my father went through but through my own experience—losing a beloved aunt to cancer five days away from her 38th birthday and a good friend of mine in a drunk driving accident in high school. It didn't make sense that a good God could sit back and make bad things happen.

An only child growing up in the farming community of Hastings, Minnesota, life was relatively uneventful. I was a good girl who got good grades, stayed out of trouble, and never gave my parents a hard time. I was a lot like my mother, Rosemary, who everyone called Rie for short—highly organized and detail-oriented.

Then junior year happened, specifically a boy. I got pregnant and became one of "those" girls. Maybe you know the kind. The ones that people wag their fingers at and say that they'll never make it. The ones that become easy targets for judgment.

Matter of fact, the day my guidance counselor, Mrs. Nelson, showed me into my first support group session for the newly created "teen mom program." I shook my head and with a hint of indignation said, "Oh no, no, no. I'm not going in there. I'm not one of them." But for the most part we were, of course, the same. Scared little girls with growing bellies and uncertain futures.

I had gotten pregnant in November, and though I knew something was amiss in my body, the first pregnancy test I took came back negative. Unconvinced, I took another test a few weeks later. And sure enough, pregnant I was. My then-boyfriend decided the right thing to do was to tell our parents together. Mine were first. The four of us sat in the family room in awkward silence. A few minutes passed before I finally blurted out, "Mom, Dad, I'm pregnant."

Eyes widened and jaws dropped. This was not news they had expected. My mother was crushed. The look in her big hazel eyes evidenced the disappointment. Not much was said that afternoon, but a day later my father bought me a gift, a baby rattle. I think he was still reeling from shock. Despite their devastation at this earth-shattering revelation, I knew my parents loved me and would support me however they could. And they did.

It took me some time to accept this reality. I remember being curled up in my bed, covered by thick, wool blankets, and praying, "Dear God, please take this situation away. Please don't make me do this." Even though I viewed Him as a distant and icy administrator of the planet, I was hopeful God would answer my prayer. Maybe He could throw some compassion my way. For Pete's sake, I was only seventeen. I had plans, big plans. I was thinking about going to college in California, and then law school. I was going to become a big time attorney and make a wad of money. A baby didn't fit into the picture. A baby meant detours and U-turns and a new landscape that didn't jibe with the vision of my life.

I continued my studies in school and once a week attended a teen mom support group. I came to love those six girls as we sat around a circle week after week hashing out our fears and concerns and sharing giggles while a counselor guided our time together. It was quite the eye-opening experience. Some girls were kicked out of their homes when their parents heard the news, others were dealing with abusive boyfriends. I used this time to vent about how lonely I felt, how my friendships had changed, how some of my so-called friends became these awkward people, not knowing how to talk to me. I was terrified at the thought of giving up my dreams and processed this fear with Mrs. Nelson.

As weeks passed, I felt more settled, confident that a baby didn't mean my life would end. If anything, this beautiful gift forced me to dream bigger because life wasn't just about me anymore. I knew being a teen mom wouldn't be easy, but I also knew with all my heart that I was supposed to be a mother. And I could do this, especially with the devoted support of my wonderful parents.

In his song "Unanswered Prayers," award-winning country artist Garth Brooks writes how some of God's greatest gifts are the prayers He doesn't answer. This song reminds me of my daughter, Samantha, who was born on August 23, 1990. I did not know love until I gave birth to my darling little girl. While I didn't have my future strategized, holding this tiny beauty in my arms, her hands curled tightly around my finger, I felt unconditional love wash over me. Life changed, all right, for the better! And I knew that somehow, some way, everything was going to be all right.

I returned to school for my senior year, ambitious and hopeful, while my parents helped care for Samantha during the day. My daughter was two months old when I ended things with my boyfriend. There's no need to include the detailed drama, but it's important to note that it was an unhealthy relationship.

Having a baby made me grow up really fast. My priority was being a good mother and provider. Sure, I wanted to go to college and get a good job, but not to give myself props.

I wanted to give Samantha the best. Besides, I couldn't live on government assistance forever. While I was grateful for the provision of welfare, it was only a means to an end until I was able to financially get by on my own two feet.

My bubbly little girl went with me everywhere. We were a package deal. I met a few guys along the way, but when they found out I was a mom, they ran off in the opposite direction. Samantha was only a few months old when I began to accept that life could very well just be the two of us, forever. And I was okay with that. Besides, I was too busy learning the challenging art of juggling school and being a mom.

* * *

After gradation I attended Inver Hills Community College on a full-ride scholarship. Enrolling in a work-study program allowed a little extra money to pay for childcare. At the end of my first year, I was asked to speak at a breakfast attended by local business owners that helped sponsor the scholarship I was awarded. The objective of this event was to highlight the importance of continuing the scholarship for future applicants. I was both honored and nervous as I shared my story in front of a room of business owners and entrepreneurs.

Around the same time, my dad and I had started attending Sunday services at a local Methodist church with a few hundred members. A dear elderly neighbor had recently passed away, and he had been a member at Hastings United Methodist Church. The love that this congregation had shown to our friend and his family during his illness drew us there. I had no prior ties to the Methodist denomination, nor did I know anything about it, but I figured it had to be a more reasonable sanctuary than our local Catholic church that I had attended every so often during my pregnancy. I felt heavily judged in that particular parish as the mother of a baby out of wedlock. I never went back. While I was wary of attending another church for fear of judgment, the Methodist church warmly greeted Dad, Samantha, and me with open arms. It was a beautiful sanctuary. The altar in the front of the church backed into beautiful stain-glass windows, which streamed light directly on the large cross on the back wall.

My father and I were immediately drawn to the loving atmosphere and to the lead pastor, Duane Sarazin, as well as Gordon Gathright, the youth pastor. Both of these leaders reflected kind, compassionate, and humble spirits. The whole experience was quite refreshing, meaningful and reflective, not stuffy and impersonal.

Ironically, Ken Linde, a businessman who had attended the breakfast where I had spoken turned out to be a good friend of Gordon (who is an incredible friend and mentor to David and me still to this day.) Ken recommended that I speak to the church youth group about teen pregnancy and peer pressure. When Gordon, a tall, burly man peppered with thinning grey hair and whose eyes always twinkled, approached me about this opportunity, I was quick to say yes, but hid some of my apprehension. I had only started going to the church, didn't even know what a "youth group" was, and had no inkling on how to stand in front of a bunch my peers and tell them about the consequences of temptation. As I meekly smiled at Gordon, after agreeing to this, fears bounced around my mind. *Would my story be helpful?*

Would the young people even listen to what I had to say? Would they even care?

But when the day came, speaking to those twenty-five teenagers changed my life. As they sprawled out on the floor and comfy couches in the church library, I shared my story of giving in to peer pressure and what life was like as a teen mom. The room was quiet while I talked, the wide-eyed youth, decked out in Air Jordans, tapered jeans, and flannel shirts, giving me their full attention. Afterwards, some of the kids came up to me and asked questions. It felt wonderful to be able pour hope and loving knowledge into their lives from an experience I initially thought would ruin my life. That day, in his characteristic inspiring and persuasive way, Gordon suckered me into volunteering with the youth as a leader every Sunday. I'll admit, I was hooked that first meeting. So it really didn't take too much persuading for me to say yes.

My faith was growing at this point. I'll never forget one Wednesday night service around the time I spoke in front of the youth for the first time. The band played a beautiful worship chorus with lyrics something like:

Oh come and sing this song with gladness
As your hearts are filled with joy
Lift your hands in sweet surrender to His name
Oh give Him all your tears of sadness
Give Him all your years of pain
And you'll enter into life in Jesus' name

I softly sang under my breath and in that moment, I felt enveloped by the love of God. It felt like He had entered my heart, not only because I prayed a prayer, but also because of my willing and wanting spirit. God had made a home in me.

As I spent more and more time with the youth, I started noticing this six-feet tall, good-looking guy with glasses who always wore cowboy boots. David Bowers was also a volunteer. Ironically, he was present at the time I spoke to the kids, but I was so absorbed in the talk and interacting with those in the room, I just hadn't paid attention to his tall, dark, and handsome self. David had a presence about him, a quiet confidence that made you feel comfortable. The youth group kids loved him. And the more I got to know him through spending time with the kids, the more I liked the guy. Problem was, I had been hurt so deeply by Samantha's biological father that I had barricaded my heart, my feelings, and my desires within carefully constructed, concrete walls.

There was also the busy factor. I didn't have time to date. I was around twenty, going to school full time, working three part-time jobs, and mothering an almost two-year-old. When could I realistically squeeze in a dinner or coffee date with some guy? Hmm, let's see. Oh yeah, the twelfth of never.

Finally, I had a daughter who I loved and adored with every part of my being. I certainly didn't expect any guy my age to swoop in on a white horse and carry me and a feisty toddler off into the sunset for a happily-ever-after existence. I had to be realistic about dating. Even though I had gone out with a few guys here and there, nothing even remotely serious developed.

And yet, David continued to pique my interest. I

knew nothing about him, so I started asking around, very discreetly, and hearing some good things. He was a hard-working and successful engineer, had his own house, and overall was just a great guy. One of the biggest things I admired was that David, this young, cool, guy actually chose not just to attend church but to serve here as well. Whenever we interacted during church events, I felt a strange mixture of feelings, vacillating from a desire to get to know him better to wanting to shut down the whole thing out of fear.

I headed down to Wisconsin to visit a friend with Amy VanVleet, a neighbor who became a close friend when I got pregnant and stuck with me during the rough times. When I got back to Minnesota, David was gone. It was quite the bummer. But it didn't take long to hear that he was at an out-of-town job site for six weeks. When he returned, much to my delight, our interactions at church became more frequent and finally, the big ask. David called me out of the blue one night and after bouncing back some small talk said, "Hey, Carly, would you like to go to a dinner and a movie Friday night?"

I paused briefly. I knew that Friday afternoon I had a doctor's appointment scheduled to get trigger point injections in my head and neck for a car accident related pain condition. I'd had them before so I knew what to expect, mainly the fact that the lower part of my face would be sore and eating would be painful. With my nerves meshing with excitement, I blurted out, "Well, I can probably see a movie, but I can't go to dinner."

"Oh," David said, sounding crestfallen.

I didn't think of how my response was going to come

across. Thinking about it now, I guess it did sound like a polite rejection. Needless to say, David and I did go to the movies. Our time together wasn't peppered with long-winded conversation, but we certainly had enough fun to go out a few more times in the next week or two. Though we were both excited about getting to know each other outside of hanging out with rambunctious teenagers at the go-kart tracks, pool parties, kick ball games, and youth services, we kept our dates private. David and I were cautious. In case we decided we were incompatible, we didn't want it to be weird within the church. But it wasn't long before word got out.

The more I got to know David, the more I fell in love. He was calm, smart, and levelheaded. I felt safe with him. I did have many talks with Gordon where I voiced my fears of pursuing this serious relationship (I found out later that David had the same kind of talks with Gordon). Mainly, it was because I was scared. But Gordon could see we were both falling in love and encouraged us in the process.

In the summer of 1993, a year after we started dating, David proposed to me at the Valleyfair amusement theme park. He and I had taken Samantha for a spin on the carousel, lit by bright lights on the ceiling and vibrant splashes of color from the majestic wooden horses. David was riding a white stallion. As the music played and the carousel circled around a few times, he leapt off his horse like a knight and stood right next to me. Then, he popped the question.

I said yes.

While the proposal didn't come with a shiny ring, he did take me shopping a few days later for—get this—a car! At that point, I had graduated Inver Hills and was attending classes at Hamline University in St. Paul for paralegal studies. My old, beat up Camaro would break down on me on practically every commute from home to school. I'm sure David was pretty tired of having to leave work early to rescue me from the side of the road. The sedan was perfect, safe, in good condition, and fit Samantha's car seat much better than my raggedy sports car. Of course I wanted a ring, but what I really needed was a car. And that gesture melted my heart more than any shiny rock would. (And yes, I did eventually get a ring, a month or so before our wedding.)

David

I grew up in Brazil...the small town community in Indiana, home to a slew of now-closed coalmines, thriving farmland, and stretched out country roads. I know, a lot less exotic than South America. My mom, Marilyn, was a wonderful cook, who stayed at home to raise my two sisters, Amber and Teresa, and me, while my Dad, Keith, a fix-it genius, worked for an agriculture-based co-op system. It seemed like he knew everyone in the county. He either sold product to them or he didn't and was very much aware of that fact.

The Methodist church was like a second home to me ever since I could remember. I found comfort there, though I wouldn't necessarily say I developed a personal relationship with God (that didn't happen until sometime in high school, when I accepted an altar call invitation at a revival service.) As a child, faith was simply ingrained in me. Going to church and serving was something I was supposed to do, like brushing my teeth or studying hard. As a kid it was hard to connect with fellow church members. Most of them were forty-plus years my senior. But despite the age gap, I learned the importance of serving others—making homemade apple cider for the local children's home, trimming trees on the property, helping to pour concrete for the church's renovations.

After graduating high school, I headed to Purdue University. There I enrolled in a co-op program where I alternated between working a semester for Union Carbide (UC) and going to school the next. I graduated from Purdue in 1991 with a degree in Mechanical Engineering. It took five years and included two years of work experience. It made sense to continue working with UC after graduation, though the company wasn't high on anyone's popularity list at the time. In Bhopal, India in 1984, 40 tons of poisonous gas leaked from a chemical plant owned by Union Carbide and killed at least ten thousand people and injured more. Though a heartbreaking tragedy, the division I was interested in at UC, which had nothing to do with the disaster, didn't seem dangerous at the time. Besides, the pay was good and I already had two years of experience with them. So when they offered me a job after graduation, I accepted and moved to Hastings, Minnesota. I worked as an engineer at a plant that produced oxygen, and as the company started downsizing, I conducted project work at other facilities for weeks at a time.

Short of working, there wasn't much to do in small town USA. I checked off the basics of finding an apartment and started looking into a more permanent living situation. I knew I had to find a church. Out came the phone book. I visited the first and only Methodist church my fingers pointed to on the yellow pages. My first Sunday, I was greeted by an older guy, named Harry, who appeared to be the head usher. After the service, in what I thought was a very thoughtful gesture, he asked me my name and some other introductory information. I had seen him earlier carrying around a notebook, but didn't notice that after our conversation, he quickly jotted down notes of who I was and where I came from. This man, with warm eyes and a smattering of gray hair, did this with every newcomer. It was his way of making sure first-time visitors felt like they mattered, that someone recognized the fact that they set foot in a new church. Because this, for most people, is not an easy thing to do.

After coming home from a long day, I didn't care much for planting myself in front of the TV or reading mindless magazines. A natural workhorse, I wanted to do something that made a difference. So I started volunteering for the church, first helping out with a renovation project. I cleaned. I sanded. I varnished. I painted. I cut. I measured. I built. I poured in a lot of sweat equity in the evening hours and enjoyed every minute of it. There I met Gordon, the youth pastor, a brawny, compassionate and fun-loving guy who convinced me to lend a hand with the youth group. I loved hanging out with the kids, but whenever Gordon would ask me to teach a lesson, it stopped being fun. I learned quickly that public speaking was not my thing.

One Wednesday night, seated in the back of the sanctuary, I started scoping out the pews. Hey, I was a single guy. And isn't church one of the best places to meet someone? I noticed a woman I hadn't seen before. Her rich brunette hair was cropped, showing off a svelte neck. Once I saw she was seated next to a man, albeit an older one, I turned away. There was no way my eyes would fall on a married woman. A week or so later, I noticed that same back of the head in youth group. Though this time, she was chatting with Gordon and getting ready to speak. Taking one look at her angelic face for the first time, I was relieved to see that this mystery lady was young. And, in hearing her talk, that she was a single teen mom, not a spring chicken married to the 50-something guy I saw her sitting next to in service, who was actually her father. I leaned against the back wall as I listened to Carly share her story of giving in to temptation in high school and life as a young mom. I was impressed. Real impressed. It wasn't only because she was beautiful—which, of course, she was. I could just tell by her mannerisms, her confidence, and her story that she was driven. She had a solid work ethic. She was working hard on not letting life or hardships drag her down. She seemed to be making lemonade out of the lemons that life had handed her. I admired that! Carly was my kind of gal.

But it took weeks for this introverted engineer to muster up the courage to ask her out. Carly talks about the walls she had built around her heart after having Samantha; I also had some of my own. I was involved in a relationship up until my junior year in college. Over the years we simply grew apart and finally went our separate ways. As much as I wanted to fall in love with my dream girl, I was cautious about pursuing another relationship. But the pull toward Carly was too strong. And finally, one day after having casual conversations with her during youth group and other church-related events, I picked up the phone and asked her out.

When Carly blurted out that she couldn't go to dinner

but maybe a movie, I was taken aback. Her excuse, which I highly doubted was legitimate, made it seem like the only reason she said a kind-of version of yes was because she felt sorry for me. Going to dinner and actually having to talk to one another in private for an hour or two seemed like way too much of a commitment for her. She might as well have told me that she needed to wash her hair.

When we finally did go out, I brought along a little gift for her. It wasn't flowers or a box of chocolates. I had heard through the church grapevine that Carly had recently made chocolate chip cookies for a youth group event. Not being the culinary artist she is today, she settled for a recipe she found on the back of a package of Tollhouse chocolate chips to make sure they'd be edible. As a group of teens started munching on the gooey goodness, one of them gushed, "Oh! These aren't David Bowers' cookies, are they?" Nope, they weren't. At the time, Carly had no idea the kids were accustomed to regularly indulging in my perfected chocolate chip cookie recipe. So on our first date, I handed her a printed recipe card of what was my mother's recipe nestled in a plastic sleeve. Hey, I had to give Carly a hard time about it; I liked her!

We took our relationship slowly, not filling in the church or youth group until we had a big oops! moment. It was a cold September day and Carly showed up to an event wearing a sweatshirt emblazoned with the word "Purdue." And that was that.

Being a part of Samantha's life was a joy and we shared an instant connection. I was glad that she was used to seeing me around regularly before Carly and I became a couple. Samantha always hung out with the kids at youth group and everyone just loved to dote on her. My parents had no reservations with me dating a woman who had a child. They trusted my instincts and had enough faith in me to respect my decisions. I'll always appreciate that.

In the summer of 1993, Carly, Samantha and I, along with twenty-four of Carly's first cousins, spent the day at the Valleyfair amusement theme park. Located on the banks of the Minnesota River, it boasts towering rollercoasters, spine-tingling thrill rides, and a waterpark that offers great relief on those dog days of summer. As we made our way through the grounds with little Samantha in a stroller between us, we passed a monstrous-sized Ferris wheel. I pointed to the stately structure, staring at the swinging pods holding the passengers. "Let's go on that," I said, playfully nudging Carly in the ribs. "I'll ask you to marry me if you do."

Carly, however, did not share my sense of adventure nor find any humor in my potential proposal. She responded with a dirty look, complete with an eye roll. (Did I mention she was afraid of heights? And that Ferris wheels freaked her out?)

Later that night, the three of us hopped on a carousel, placing a squealing Samantha on a black horse draped in pastel colors. While carnival music played in the background, I hopped off my seat and stood next to Samantha. Looking at Carly, who had her arm around the little girl, I asked her to marry me. This time, she took me seriously. And, well, by now, you know what she said.

Union Carbide was falling apart internally, selling off divisions of the company. The air separation division where I worked eventually became Praxair. The company offered me a new position as a Process Control engineer at their engineering headquarters in Tonawanda, New York, a town about fifteen minutes from Buffalo. I'd be responsible for maintaining the systems that operated some plants around the country. Not long after Carly and I would exchange our vows, we would need to pack up, say goodbye to dear friends and family, and head up to New York.

Carly

David and I got married on July 2, 1994, a year after we got engaged. It was a simple, intimate affair with a lot of personal touches. Gordon's daughter sang a song. The youth group kids helped with communion. During the ceremony, David gave Samantha, almost four at the time, a ring of her own and asked if he could be her dad. We honeymooned at a bed and breakfast near Lake Superior, enjoying candlelight dinners, long walks around the lighthouse, nearby museums, and romantic sunsets where bursts of golden orange color blanketed the sky. A day or two after we got home, moving vans were parked outside David's house. My parent's house was next.

I knew that moving came with the territory of my husband's job. I signed up for this when I married him. Still, it was hard to say goodbye to the life I had made for myself and my daughter, which included the wonderful church we called home, the amazing kids we led who had become dear to our hearts, my parents who had been such a tremendous support for me after having Samantha, and Gordon, who had led me into faith with his shining example and compassionate spirit. Tears were shed the day the three of us left. A lot of tears. As much as I knew this was the plan, I was afraid of leaving the familiar.

David, Samantha, and I settled into an apartment in Cheektowaga, a suburb of Buffalo and then moved a bit later to East Aurora, the home of Fischer Price. Pretty quickly, my initial perspective of the move shifted into something of an adventure. Oh, I still had some fears, but for the most part I was excited starting off somewhere new as a new family. In hindsight, it was probably the best thing for us. I had become somewhat dependent on my parents and now being so far away, I couldn't run to them if I had a problem. I had to figure out glitches and hiccups on my own, which is what you need to do as a married adult. As a result of the distance, my marriage to David grew strong.

We stayed in New York for eighteen months, which included two very long winters. One 24-hour storm dumped a record-breaking 38 inches of snow in the area, leaving much of our town paralyzed. Another year, we had so much snow one Easter, David and I were able to build Samantha a 7-foot snow bunny. Harsh winters aside, we were quick to embrace the local church community, plugging into one a few blocks away from our new home. David and I started volunteering with the youth group and eventually led a small group ministry (and in the process made many desperate "help us" phone calls to Pastor Gordon for guidance and resources). While Samantha was in preschool, I attended the State University of New York-Buffalo, taking classes in sociology and legal studies, while working at a pizza joint to make ends meet.

One of the most memorable events of being in Buffalo

was that David began (and eventually completed) the process of adopting Samantha. She absolutely adored him and it just melted my heart that he, since the day we married, has considered her to be his own.

And then, it was time to leave again.

David

While I love working in the trenches as an engineer, being stuck in a cubicle wearing a shirt and tie was suffocating. But that was part of my job in New York. Instead of being in the field, I was managing, troubleshooting and finding solutions for the computer communication aspect in facilities throughout the country (think dial-up modems). Moving around so much was quite a challenge, but the only way to accelerate career-wise at Praxair was to build hands-on experience. And that meant bouncing around the country when particular jobs became available. After spending eighteen months in New York, I got transferred to Texas, a world away from whipping winds, dipping temperatures, and vicious snowstorms.

As a production superintendent, I was responsible for ensuring the plant was up and running 24/7. This involved a fair share of troubleshooting, project planning, management, maintenance, and helping supervise a seven-man team. I worked for Clyde, a great guy with admirable leadership qualities who had a knack for taking care of his guys. Our team worked such long and hard hours, one way we dealt with the stress was getting creative with meal planning. There were days we'd make ice cream from nitrogen, roast a good cut of beef in the welding rod oven, or cook some beans over a hot plate. I enjoyed the camaraderie we had as a team and with Clyde, who naturally fostered a spirit of fellowship and togetherness. It made for a great working environment.

Hitching our wagon to a faith community was a priority for our family. But the things we wanted in a church were changing. While the one we attended in New York was big, we weren't much interested in numbers. We wanted to see how a church was impacting its family as well as the community. Driving around town one day, we found Wesley United Methodist Church. It was definitely a lot smaller than what we were used to, and while we were willing to give it a try, Carly and I shared a smidgen of doubt that they would have as many programs or resources as our other churches. Maybe because of their size, their community outreach would be limited. Boy, were we wrong!

Carly

We started attending a local church, a smaller one than we were accustomed to but one that had big vision. I liked that. As we dove into volunteering, there was plenty of room for David and I to pioneer and grow certain programs. Eventually, the church offered me a part-time position as a youth leader, designing and planning lessons. I loved pouring into the lives of these kids, loving on them, creating fun and unique lessons and activities for them. And what a blessing to be able to serve and minister alongside my husband.

Though after having Samantha, I was motivated to finish my college education, something changed when I got married. I became a lot more domestic. I'll never forget when David and I were dating, after church one Sunday Samantha and I headed to his house to make brunch. I rummaged through his cupboards and pantry like a mad-woman and finally, exasperated, asked David where he kept the Bisquick. David looked at me funny and shook his head. "Oh, no, no, no, Carly," he said. "Open the fridge and get out the buttermilk." I froze on the spot. *Good lord,* I thought, *I'm doomed.* As much as I loved being a mom, I was not Betty Crocker or Martha Stewart. I'd rather bury my face in books than make a roast or polish silverware.

But while the State University of New York allowed me in-state tuition fees, which was a lot less money than pay-ing out-of-state costs, Texas wouldn't extend that same courtesy. So my plan to attend Lamar University was nixed. David and I decided to have a baby instead. Nathan was born on March 26, 1997. Life with baby number two was different than the first. With Samantha, I felt like I had to get back into the swing of things rather quickly. I needed to finish school, make plans for my future, and figure life out practically the minute I gave birth. With Nathan, I could sit on the couch for hours holding him, staring at him, soak-ing in his coos, gurgles, and giggles. I didn't watch a clock or worry about making goal timelines. I enjoyed the rolling waves of a life absent of stringent schedules.

Life was good. My husband was moving up in his com-pany. We had two healthy, beautiful children. We were involved in a loving community of faith.

Does it get any better?

That's what I wondered not but a week or two before

David's accident, before the future we were building disintegrated. It's like what Hugh Prathner wrote, "Just when I think I have learned the way to live, life changes.[3]" Sometimes for the better. Sometimes for the worse.

And sometimes, it's a beautiful and heartbreaking marriage of both.

3.

What life means to us is determined not so much by what life brings us as by the attitude we bring to life; not so much by what happens to us as by our reaction to what happens.[4]

Lewis Dunnington

Carly

Maybe the doctors were wrong.

Maybe they didn't know what they were doing, what they were talking about.

I chewed my lip and stared out the window while Lynne, our pastor, drove me two and a half hours to UTMB Galveston. Jackie Philyaw had offered to take care of Samantha and Nathan back at the house so I could be with David and the kids could maintain as much of a normal life as realistically possible.

My thoughts raced as Lynne and I sped down unfamiliar highways, following Clyde and Linda who drove in another car leading us to Galveston. A part of me believed that once we got to this renowned burn center, the doctors would have a better grasp of David's injuries, a more positive picture than the ER doctors had at St. Mary's. I tried to convince myself that these new physicians would encourage me that my husband was fine, slapping me on the back with a smile and saying it wasn't as bad as anticipated. That all David needed was some cleaning and bandaging, maybe some antibiotics or something. And that he'd be able to come home in a few days' time.

Wishful thinking.

My mind quickly jumped from hoping for a misdiagnosis to fearing a more dismal outlook. Tears fell as I mourned the potential loss of my husband, the father of our two amazing children. It's dumbfounding—the mental gymnastics your emotions go through when you wander into unknown territory, ill equipped, without any direction, blindly swatting your way through the dark.

Who would teach Nathan how to catch a ball?

Who was going to walk Samantha down the aisle when she got married?

Who was going to help me parent two young children?

And then, in another mental turn, prayer. In silence, I reached out to God. *Lord, give me the chance to see David again. Please.*

Sensing my wrestling match with doubt and fears, Lynne turned to me and said, "Carly, when you pray, you have to pray with faith. Cast aside the doubt. And believe that God will hear and answer your prayers."

I nodded, tears streaming down my face. Lynne and I prayed much of the way. Sometimes out loud, sometimes in our hearts, where words were few but emotions deep and plenty. Outside of those prayers, more phone calls were made on the drive. A village of support, family, friends from church, co-workers, were all making their way to the hospital. After many failed attempts at getting in touch with David's parents, Keith and Marilyn, I finally got a hold of his youngest sister, Amber, who told us they were away on a business trip with their co-op community in Chicago. We would later learn that they had been traveling on a bus around the time of the accident. By the time they reached their destination and heard the news, someone had already made arrangements for them to fly down to Galveston to be with their son. David's sisters, Amber and Teresa, were scheduled to arrive in the morning. My parents, Chuck and Rie, David's college buddy Rob, and Gordon were also on their way.

Lynne and I had to board the Galveston-Port Bolivar ferry from Highway 87 in order to get to UTMB campus. The diesel-powered ferry, capable of carrying 52 cars and 400 passengers, wasn't just a mode of transportation taking me from point A to point B, though I didn't know it at the time. It would also be a link transitioning me from wife mode to mom mode. For the next four months, I'd trade these hats regularly, taking care of my husband on one end of the island and my kids over on the mainland. And I'd feel the torrent of guilt every time I'd put one hat down and pick the other up.

The hospital campus was an 84-acre maze of individual medical buildings, research centers, clinics, and parking decks. Someone had given me directions to the burn unit in the John Sealy hospital, but by the time we parked and, along with Clyde and Linda, scrambled our way through a labyrinth of long walkways, short hallways and elevators, we still felt lost, especially without appropriate hospital signage and a concrete sense of direction. Finally, we stood in front of two giant electric doors, hoping we were at the right location. I shrugged and pressed the button to open the doors. Turns out, we were right.

After walking down a short and relatively empty corridor, a nurse greeted us kindly but quickly. "The doctors are working on your husband right now, Mrs. Bowers. It will take quite a bit of time, but they'll come out and give you an update when they can." She made pretty clear by the tone of her voice that we'd have to sit tight for a while.

The nurse ushered the four of us into the family waiting room, directly across from another electronic doorway that opened to the actual eight-bed burn unit. It would be hours before I could see David and receive an idea of the extent of his injuries, most importantly, whether or not he would survive. Though I already was well aware that the current odds painted a terrible picture.

Those hours were excruciating though I was grateful for the company and support of good friends. I know now that the nurses and doctors were busy, performing grueling medical procedures to keep my husband alive, but to sit in a room for hours without even hearing a peep of an update? I felt out of control, on the verge of losing the most important man in my life. It would have meant the world for someone to sweep in and give me a glimpse into the unknown, into what I was facing. Was it death? Life? Something in between? Without any knowledge, I was left to my own devices, battling my imagination of fears and worse case scenarios with faith and prayers.

David

I was heavily sedated when I arrived at the Burn Intensive Care Unit (BICU). And I pretty much stayed that way for the first few days.

Even when I was conscious during the next four months as a patient in the burn unit, I was sedated, sometimes heavily, particularly after surgeries. I would later learn that while most burn units follow similar protocols of care, some choose to put severely burned patients into medically induced comas to allow them to undergo the painful recovery process while unconscious. And for good reason. For most, the pain is intolerable. One of the nurses in the hospital had said, "The pain for a burn patient is like continuous torture. It just doesn't end." So knocking them out for a time seems humane. It tends to make caring for a patient and performing the endless amounts of physically grueling medical procedures easier for both the staff and the patient.

Other burn units, however, do not share this philosophy. The burn unit at UTMB did not put me in a coma. So while I was unconscious at first, it didn't take long for me to become aware of my surroundings and observe what was happening to my body, even though this happened over a time and in bits and pieces. While bearing the brunt of agonizing pain certainly wasn't fun, being awake for the most part helped me, to a large degree, process my recovery and force me to face a my new life before I was discharged. Looking back, being conscious was a blessing in disguise. It gave me somewhat of a sense of control over my situation. Which, as an engineer, was very important.

That being said, I was still heavily sedated, pumped up with morphine and other pain-relieving drugs, so I dozed in and out of routine consciousness during much of my stay. Due to the medication, there were plenty of times my mind went haywire, hallucinating crazy things and coming up with illogical, but very rational to me at the time, theories about my care and the intentions of those caring for me. But I'll get to that later.

Keeping all this in mind, my telling of our story for the next few months will be brief and intermittent. What I write is a mix of hazy memories, medical records, journals filled in by my wife, and post-discharge conversations. There are many days I don't remember and some that I do, though a good deal of these remind me of the movie *Groundhog Day*.

But something I'll never forget is the tub room.

Akin to a torture chamber, it's where I spent the first few hours upon arriving at the burn center. Thankfully, I was unconscious and also don't remember the first few rounds in this highly despised and necessary burn unit staple. The tub room consists of a shower table, complete with nozzles and hoses containing water, as well as a giant tub with an obnoxiously noisy rail and chain mechanism that helps hoist patients inside. Burn patients either lay on the shower table or get in the tub while nurses and doctors debride the skin, remove the unhealthy or dead tissue off the body. This was the first thing that needed to be done to determine how bad my burns were. Then, my skin was basically scrubbed clean with a water and bleach solution to prevent infection.

In order for a third-degree burn to become healthy, the damaged skin must be debrided and cleaned every single day to remove the dead skin and get to healthy tissue. The only parts of my body that were not severely burned were my ankles, feet and beltline, as they'd been protected by my leather boots and belt. Everything else was a charred mess. The nurses had their work cut out for them that day and days moving forward, as they began to clean up and debride my burned body with a washcloth. As soft as cotton is, it felt like a wire brush scraping my skin. You get where I'm going with this torture chamber thing?

Getting scrubbed clean of dead skin wasn't the only thing that took place when I was first admitted. Swelling is a major issue with severe burns. My body ballooned two times its normal size and as a result, I was at a major risk not just for tissue, organ and nerve damage, but also for functional compromise of my limbs. As my body started getting grossly engorged, doctors had to perform emergency escharotomies, which look as scary as they sound. A series of deep incisions were made along the length of my arms, sides of my neck, abdomen, and legs, releasing the pressure from the swelling, allowing for expansion, and preventing further damage.

Large three-degree burns wreak havoc on your whole body, messing up all the systems and organs that are supposed to work together to keep you healthy and alive. The skin is the largest organ in the body. It regulates your body temperature and holds in fluids. When serious burns occur, you lose that protection and your body starts leaking necessary fluid that will need to be replenished intravenously or you will go into shock, organ failure, and die. So aside from the scrubbing, cleaning, and cutting, I was also pumped full of fluids. Needless to say, a lot was happening in that infamous tub room, unbeknownst to me or my dear wife, who waited anxiously in the waiting room.

Hurricane Bret was approaching the Texas coastline a day or so after my accident. Watches and warnings were being posted and residents were advised to take necessary precautions. Some parts of the coast were even ordered to evacuate. I had always wanted to live through a hurricane. I know, odd, but even engineers have an adventurous side. And there I was, lying unconscious in a hospital burn unit as rain and wind violently battled over the ocean. By the time Hurricane Bret made landfall, it had weakened, though the local area suffered some beach erosion. Just as well. I had my own storm to contend with.

Carly

It was hours before a doctor showed up. One look at his face and the little hope that had lingered on the car ride to the hospital vanished. The outlook was obviously bleak.

"Your husband has a high mortality injury," he began as I nodded somewhat impatiently. Déjà vu from the emergency room at St. Mary's.

"David was burned over 94% of his body, 76% of which are severe, third-degree burns."

I nodded, the lump in my throat growing bigger as I forced myself not to burst out in tears. I listened with a mixture of devastation and numbness as he offered an equation used by the medical field to assess the likelihood of death in burn patients.

"First we take the age of the patient, in David's case 31, and add that to the percentage of burns, which is 94."

Now, I've never been a genius at arithmetic, but even I could do the math. This doctor, this burn expert, was telling me that there was a 125% chance that my husband would die.

"The first 72 hours are critical," the doctor warned. "We'll have to wait and see how David progresses." And with that, he walked back into the tub room, which just happened to be the next room over, to continue working on my husband.

The tears fell as I collapsed on a couch in the waiting room, Lynne by my side, Clyde and Linda on nearby chairs, stunned yet still whispering prayers.

"Don't focus on the statistic, Carly," Lynne encouraged. "Focus on prayer. Focus on hope. Instead of wrestling with doubt and fear, put your trust in the Lord. Trust Him like the Psalmist did, with your whole heart, your whole soul, your whole mind."

It seemed like a gargantuan task at the time, but she was right. The more I thought about that equation, the more depressed, anxious, and panicked I became.

Trust in the Lord.

I sighed, bowing my head as my friend and pastor wrapped her arm tight around me.

Help me to do that, God, I prayed. *Help me to trust in You.*

Another hour passed and another doctor, a tall, fit man with sandy-blonde hair, walked into the room. Quiet with a gentle disposition and a prominent dimple in his right cheek, Dr. Arthur Sanford, a recently appointed burn surgeon who would become the lead physician on David's case, spoke briefly and to the point. He regurgitated the same information as the previous doctor—that my husband's odds of survival were slim, and it was a waiting game to get a better picture of his prognosis. He wasn't a chatterbox, but concisely answered our questions, like he was giving us just enough information. Dr. Sanford also mentioned that while there was no evidence that David's lungs were damaged from the explosion he cautioned that that type of injury is likely to show up within twenty-four to forty-eight hours. In other words, it was only a matter of time before David was hit with another life-threatening concern.

* * *

At this point, a couple of kids from youth group, including Big Nate and Ashley, who had also babysat for us many times, were at our house watching over Samantha and Nathan. Irene and Cindy, friends from church were also there helping out. I felt relieved knowing our children were in good hands. I didn't care if they were up past midnight or gorging on potato chips or bouncing off the walls. I only cared they were loved on and distracted from the weight of circumstances they were unable to understand, let alone carry.

Elie Wiesel, Auschwitz survivor and author of the best-selling book *Night*, wrote, "Just as despair can come to one only from other human beings, hope, too, can be given to one only by other human beings."[5] While I relied heavily on my faith, I also clung to the prayers that were lifting up our family. Prayers that were whispered in the waiting room. Prayer vigils were taking place at our church back home and by people in other states, in other countries, even from those who barely knew us. There were many moments, that night and going forward, that I actually felt the power of the prayers as these people, near and far, held me up.

During the hours it took for a doctor to fill me in on my husband's condition, Team David set up shop in the waiting room. At first, Lynne, Clyde, and his wife Linda sat beside me, offering words of comfort, prayers and sometimes the most effective, presence in the midst of silence. But as time passed, more people piled in. There was as many as twenty loved ones in the waiting room at one point. Our dear friend Jackie came as quickly as she could, after she made sure our kids were settled at our house, as well as some of David's co-workers. My parents and David's parents arrived later that night along with Gordon, and David's sisters in the morning. More family members and friends turned up over the week, packing the room with support, thoughts, prayers.

Clyde, true to his thoughtful and forward-thinking nature, took care of things. Before I knew it, he had plugged in a coffee pot into the wall on a table, assembled a tray of snacks on another table, placed a cooler filled with ice and drinks in one corner, and piled up a load of blankets and pillows in another. He was always assessing what we needed and getting it done, whether gathering supplies for the growing crowd or making phone calls. Marilyn Myers, a gal from church, told me she set up a prayer chain via email, which at the time was a relatively new technological concept for the average person. The first email she sent out was a mere three hours from the explosion.

"David Bowers has been very seriously burned at work. He has been burned over 90% of his body. Please pray for him. He is at this moment being life-flighted to Galveston. Pastor Lynne is driving Carly there now. Please pray."

Dubbed DBUs, or Dave Bowers Updates, these email notifications and prayer requests were sent out to a list of people that grew from about thirty to hundreds, spanning across the globe. In the next few days, as I read encouragement from people I knew and strangers from faraway places like India, I was filled with much gratitude and hope. What a blessing knowing so many people are praying for you and your family.

While I appreciated the stream of support and the presence of loved ones, there were times during those 72 hours where I felt I had to construct a strong front. Be brave. Not cry. Show the world I was doing fine. But there were moments I wanted nothing more than to be by myself. So I'd take my Bible and quietly head down an empty hallway in the unit, quiet except for the echo of my footsteps. Sometimes I'd plant myself on the linoleum floor or keep walking and allow the tears to fall without restraint. It felt good to have a cry fest in private. And it was what I needed many times. The tears were cathartic. It helped release the tension of trying to be a rock for my family, for everyone in the waiting room.

* * *

By the time David was settled into his room in the BICU after spending hours in the tub room, I was finally able to see him. I had been awake for hours, the cocktail of adrenaline, worry, and hope coursing through my veins. Led by a nurse, I walked out of the family waiting room and through a set of electronic doors that opened to the eight patient rooms, a nurses' station, a break room and other smaller rooms and closets housing medical supplies and such. I noticed a small desk outside the glass doors of each of the patient rooms, where one nurse, assigned to one or two patients, depending on the extent of their injuries, would sit 24/7 to monitor and chart patients' progress.

Because David was particularly susceptible to infection, before I entered his room, I had to wash up and put on a full-length gown and latex gloves. I'd have to do this every single time. The room was small, cramped. There was barely enough room for me and the nurses to flit in and out of the room without knocking into one another.

Huge machines encircled David's bed, ventilators, IV monitors, and two towering heat lamps over his bed. A trash bin was in one corner and another bin for soiled gowns occupied space in another corner, supply carts of medicine, gauze, and other essentials in another. Behind the bed stretched the only window. The lack of natural light seemed depressing, but one of the nurses later told me the hospital was built with a hurricane-resistant design, thus the absence of many windows.

The room smelled terrible, a putrid mix of burned flesh, blood, and antiseptic. I was apprehensive walking into the tiny space full of machines, wires, IVs, and more medical equipment than I'd ever seen in my life. My heart raced in the second or two before I stood by David's bedside, staring at the tubes that were pumping fluids and pain medication into his frail body. He was still sedated, so he could neither talk nor hear me. He was also almost unrecognizable, as his body had swelled to twice its normal size, his face resembling an inflated balloon. When my eyes first fell on the unbandaged parts of his body, they looked raw, red, and bleeding, like he didn't have any skin left.

Probably what was most unsettling were the long and deep slits down every limb on his body from what doctors told me were emergency escharotomies. Because David's body was so swollen, the cuts looked even deeper, like you could easily stick your hand right into them. My heart ached for my husband. He was so physically mangled, it was a miracle he had survived this long. I didn't need a doctor to tell me this.

I remember the room being hot. Like wearing-a-fur-coat-in-the-sweltering-heat-on-a-sunny-and-humid-Texas-summer-day hot. Heat lamps were positioned over David and the heat in the room was turned up anywhere from 85 to 100 degrees. Severely burned patients can't regulate their body temperature, so it's important to keep them as warm as possible so their core temperature doesn't drop. Ironically, I had issues with heat stroke as a teenager, but being in that scorching room didn't affect me in the least. I considered that a miracle.

While David may not have been a feast for the eyes, I was so happy to see him. Oh sure, my husband was scarred beyond belief, breathing with the help of a ventilator, and virtually skinless—but he was alive and I completely understood the doctors' warning to "wait and see," but I felt hopeful. Scared and full of questions, but nonetheless hopeful.

The doctors who worked on David were tight-lipped about his prognosis pretty much the entire time he was there. They never told me anything more than I needed to know, which for the most part was whatever was happening to my husband in the present moment—whether his vitals were stable, or he needed a number of skin grafts, or he presented with a fever. There was no long-term game plan. David just had to get through this critical period hour by hour.

One of the doctors explained what had been done to David in the tub room. My eyes were wide as I pictured almost every inch of my husband's body being scraped clean of dead skin for hours. I knew it was a necessary medical procedure, but it seemed ghastly, like torture.

* * *

David's condition fluctuated drastically during the critical first few days. He would be fine in the morning, be dying at lunch due to infections, decrease in body temperature, a loss of or excess fluids, shock or swelling, and by the time the sun would set, he'd be stable again. It was jarring. One minute I'd be hopeful, the next praying desperate prayers for him to live. Getting him the right antibiotics proved both an art and a science. Biochemists were in and out of his room, creating custom cocktails after one drug or another wouldn't cut it.

When I wasn't in David's room, I was in the waiting room, flanked by David's parents, mine, other loved ones and friends. Doctors would come in every now and then, a clipboard with stacks of consent forms under their arms.

Sign this. Sign that. Sign this. Sign that.

I read through the papers, the vowels and consonants smudging into one another because of the complexities and doom and gloom mood of the medical language. If I said "yes" to this drug or that procedure, I could be saying yes to a number of scary complications, death included. But if I said "no," death would be the inevitable outcome. It was overwhelming, to say the least. I felt like David's life was not just in the doctors' hands, but also mine, through the power of the pen. But I knew I didn't have a choice. My husband needed the treatment, especially his first and upcoming surgery on Monday, where doctors would do more cleaning, cutting down to healthy tissue, as well as covering his body with cadaver skin in order to fight off and prevent infection.

Because John Sealy is a teaching hospital, I sometimes found it difficult to get information out of the doctors, not just during the first few days but for the entire length of David's stay. I didn't understand what was going on. I'd never had experience with any person who had a severe burn and was clueless on what to expect in a day in the life of a burn unit. I learned early on to be my husband's advocate, not to wait to receive information but to take a more aggressive approach. I remember the first few days when an entourage of doctors—interns and residents that rotated each month and were led by an attending physician—would come through David's room during rounds (think *Grey's Anatomy* or *House*), I'd camp right outside my husband's door and corner one of the doctors, asking questions, before the gang took off.

Mainly, I relied a lot on the nurses, especially at night when the pace was slower and they weren't stretched as thin. I peppered them nonstop with a machine gun success of questions.

"What's that tube for?"

"Why is this machine beeping?"

"Why does that body part look like this?"

"If David survives, what is life going to look like?"

They were angels, answering my questions with patience. They managed a delicate balance of offering hope and setting a realistic picture. That's a hard thing to do, believe me. When David started regaining consciousness about two or three days after the accident, hope started turning up in little ways. The first time his eyes opened and I was able to interact with him, he didn't say a word but simply followed me with his eyes. They looked tired, as if they'd come back from a bloody battlefield, but to me they were signs of life, evidence that he was still here. And more than just a beating heart and brain activity. Beneath the scarring and bandages and tubes and wires, my husband, heart, soul, mind, and spirit, was with me.

"Honey, can you wiggle your toes for me?" I asked, my hand on the steel bedside rail, as I was not allowed to touch him. Tears fell down my face when his perfectly healthy toes squirmed.

Miracle. Blessing. Hope.

Still—here came that reality check again—David wasn't out of the woods. Doctors made sure to let me know that, tempering much of my optimism with their bleak "wait and watch" reports.

"David's recovery process is going to be a long road," one doctor told us. "We've only just begun."

On August 23rd, three days after the accident and the day of David's first surgery, I woke up in the hospital waiting room, back and neck aching from the uncomfortable chairs. Still bleary-eyed and exhausted, I remembered it was Samantha's ninth birthday. My heart sank. Though I made sure the birthday party we had painstakingly planned for three days from now was scheduled to move forward, David and I wouldn't be there.

"I'm so sorry Daddy and I won't be there to celebrate your big day," I said, choking back tears.

"Don't worry, Mom, it's okay," she consoled me on the other end of the receiver. "I'll just wait for you guys. Take care of Daddy."

"Okay, baby," I said, grateful my little girl couldn't see the stream of tears or guilt scrawled over my face. That day, my father and cousins from Minnesota went back to the house and took her out to Olive Garden, her favorite restaurant. A few days later, my parents and a couple of aunts and my grandmother went back again and took her to the swim party, where her friends from church and school celebrated at her birthday bash.

I knew Samantha was being loved on and cared for, but I couldn't help but feel I was neglecting her in some way through being at the hospital this long. My daughter was (and still is) a tough cookie, and she wasn't about to cry or put up any kind of fuss. She stayed strong, even on one of the most special days of the year while her life was shifting upside down, making sure I knew she was okay. But none of us are that strong on our own. It's only a matter of time before our defensive garrisons come crumbling down. Though it wouldn't happen for a while, Samantha was no exception.

Before David's surgery I read Scripture to him as friends and family gathered, tightly squeezed, in David's room. A talented tenor, Gordon led an impromptu worship service by singing two of David's favorite hymns, "How Great Thou Art" and "Amazing Grace." The Spirit of God was so clearly felt in that room. And right before David was whisked away to surgery, I saw him turn his head and move his eyes. To me, it was confirmation that God was not just present, but active. Reminding us that despite the doctor's grim reports, He was working in and through my husband.

As I'd do during all of his surgeries, I waited and prayed back in the family waiting room, hoping to get an occasional update from the nurses. Every once in a while I'd take a short walk to get something to eat or drink. I never strayed far from the BICU just in case.

The surgery lasted five and a half hours. Because there was so little healthy tissue available to perform adequate grafts from David's body, some of the burns on his legs, fingers, arms and chest were temporarily covered with homografts, sheets of cadaver skin. In the meantime, post-age-stamp-sized samples of David's healthy tissue had been sliced off and mailed to a magical lab in Boston where biologists could use it to grow cultured skin that would later be placed over parts of his body. This is a very expensive and detailed procedure where skin is created in different stages over a period of time. Because of the costly and time-consuming process, the lab calls the hospital every few days to make sure the patient receiving the new cells is still alive. Morbid, right? This is just another sign of how fatal severe burns can be.

The first surgery went well, which meant primarily that David had lived through it. During the surgery, it was expected that David would lose a lot of blood, but the nine liters he lost was on the high end. The average human body only has six liters of the stuff. Part of the DBUs Marilyn mailed out included a request for anyone who shared

David's blood type to donate. Email after email poured in from the Team David community committing to give blood.

My emotions after surgery, all of David's surgeries for that matter, were generally mixed. On one hand, I felt relieved he survived the next surgical step. On the other hand, knowing it wasn't his last surgery brought on a surge of anxiety and worry. He got through one, but there would be others. In fact, by the time David left the BICU to enter the rehab hospital he'd undergo about eleven major surgeries, not including the multiple procedures done in the tub room. And while the worry was an expected human reaction—I'm a woman, not a robot—I found comfort in prayer, my desperate pleas intermingled with words of loved ones, friends, and strangers. We were all pulling together, unified by praying to God that David would get and stay well. And I couldn't do much else, except pray, hope, and wait.

Pray. Hope. Wait.

Repeat.

4.

Carly

Even though David was on a lot of pain medication, two or three days after he was admitted to the BICU, he was beginning to respond. Though the signs were small, considering his uncertain prognosis they were truly grand strides. Like a day before his first surgery, when David started flailing his arms after my cousin Bernadette said she was going to take his truck. Or when he blinked repeatedly after a nurse told him he was handsome. These were all signs of life, evidence of hope surfacing. I clung to these moments, held them close and continued to pray that as days crawled by and my husband stayed alive, more would follow.

On August 25, David's breathing tube came out, though doctors were still cautious as to the state of his lungs. This was more so a test run. For almost two hours, David breathed on his own for the first time since the accident after which the tube was reinserted. Doctors did this for several days, trying to wean him off the ventilator and lessen the risk of pneumonia.

I could tell the simple act of David's independent breathing boosted the doctors' confidence. My faith rose as well. I don't remember when exactly it was but it may have been around this time when some doctor confirmed David had not suffered any lung injury. It rarely happens, if ever, that a person with such severe burns recovers without any lung damage from an explosion. Looking back, when David jumped off that ladder just as the flash fire erupted, he remembered to hold his breath. It's amazing how something so simple can end up serving as a lifesaver.

When David spoke for the first time, after a final round of intubation, his hoarse, breathy voice was music to my ears. As doctors hovered around my husband, a cluster of beeping machines surrounding him, the hospital bed splayed with wires and tubes, one of the them told me, "While David is still breathing well on his own, I'm not yet entirely comfortable without him having some sort of ventilator. So we're going to go ahead and put the breathing tube back in, but this time through his nose."

I was disappointed. But not as much as David was.

It was a faint whisper, but as the doctors bounced back some medical jargon to one another, the monitors continued to drone, and nurses shuffled in here and there, David piped up in his raspy voice, "I don't think this is a good idea."

Every single person in that room busted out laughing. It almost felt like a relief, like David of all people had released this balloon of tension and re-inflated the mood in the room with a lightness. A lightness that only someone with his optimism, dry sense of humor, and wit could bring.

Though David could now talk, he wasn't a gab machine. Oh, there were days where he was lucid enough to carry on conversations longer than a few minutes, but there were an equal amount of talks where a lot of what he said didn't make sense. But what do you expect from a guy loaded up on pain meds? Either way, it didn't matter. I devoured the gibberish as much as I drank in his more meaningful words like "I love you" and "How are the kids?"

I remember talking to a nurse or a doctor about the hospital's policy not to place burn patients in medically induced comas. I was grateful for that. If I had to spend four months not being able to interact with my husband, it would have killed me. I didn't care if he didn't remember what we talked about the next day. Or the fact that we couldn't carry out hours and hours of philosophical conversations every single day. The mere fact that he was awake and able to communicate was encouraging.

Back on the home front, past the hulky freighters crawling through the Port Bolivar/Galveston waterway, the cluster of seagulls squawking for food off the stern of the crossing ferries, and down the long stretch of Highway 87, Nathan and Samantha were at the house in Nederland, being watched over by loving friends. My daughter was itching to see her dad. I could hear the desperation in her voice whenever we chatted on the phone. She asked about seeing her dad every single time, stammering amidst falling tears and trying so hard to temper her little girl sobs. I had repeatedly told her the same thing, "You'll see Daddy, soon, baby. I promise. Real soon."

But at this point, it wasn't enough. Soon needed to be now. I was nervous and felt inept in how exactly to make that happen. I wasn't as concerned about the logistics, particularly needing to get special clearance for Samantha to spend time with her dad because children were not allowed in the BICU. I was worried more about her reaction. Would she be able to handle seeing her once healthy and active and mobile dad lying on a hospital bed, burned and bandaged and unable to do much more than move his head and whisper a few things? How do I even prepare her for the scene of wires and tubes and machines and the entourage of nurses and doctors constantly cycling in and out of his room?

One of the nurses had recommended Samantha talk to a therapist named Regina who worked for Child Life Services at the adjacent Children's Hospital and who dealt with these kinds of issues. I scheduled an appointment for August 28th, only eight days after the accident. When Regina introduced herself to my daughter and me at our first appointment, we both fell in love with this compassionate woman who had an innate talent for teaching with kindness and care. Regina spent over an hour with Samantha in the family waiting room just across the hall from the BICU. She introduced my little girl to a muslin cloth doll that she was able to "fix up" with gauze, Ace bandages, and heart electrodes, just like her daddy. I watched as Samantha methodically took painstaking care of this little doll, making sure her bandages were wrapped tight enough, but not too tight, and whispering words of encouragement to the plaything that "everything is going to be okay." Regina also showed my girl pictures of the machines in David's room, explaining in simple, childlike terms the role of each gizmo. Finally, she offered Samantha a Polaroid view of David's room from the doorway.

And then, the big moment.

When it was time to see David, Samantha, gowned and gloved, clutched my hand and took a cautious step toward where her father lay, and paused. But she didn't linger there long. When their eyes locked, a smile that stretched east to west beamed on her face. She practically skipped toward him, still grinning.

Nurse Mary, a brunette who always wore a brightly patterned bandana as a headband, who we affectionately started to call "crazy Mary" paying homage to her wild and funny personality, said to David, "Samantha is here to see you."

In his playfully teasing manner he quipped from the bed, "Samantha who?"

"Your daughter!" Mary exclaimed, furrowing her eyebrows and wagging a menacing finger in David's face.

"Oooh," David said, purposely drawing out the word. "You mean my daughter Samantha who I haven't seen in days, right?" Our little girl squealed in delight, standing by her father's bedside. Without missing a beat, she started spouting a cheery monologue, complete with excited hand gestures, about her birthday party, what was going on at school, the stuff she was learning. And right before it was time to leave the room she said, "Daddy, I want to let you know that all the kids in school are praying for you. So be strong! And I love you, Daddy."

That few-minute interaction was a healing experience for both Samantha and David. They both needed to know each other was okay. Though David was bandaged, connected to IVs, and encircled by machines, his playful spirit engaged and comforted Samantha. She left with that same beaming smile on her face. And David? Seeing his girl communicate with him the same playful way she always had, without a flood of tears, without haunting questions, without an emotional eruption of fear or worry made him feel better. It was proof that his little girl was okay. She would get through this. We all would.

While I was grateful that seeing Samantha was able to lift his spirits, the thought of not being able to alleviate his physical pain was heartbreaking. I felt helpless. I was swinging on a pendulum of mixed emotions while dealing with the logistics of insurance paperwork, consent forms, and managing our home from two and a half hours away. I was trying to make sure our children were healthy, happy, and taken care of, but I wasn't the burn survivor. I wasn't undergoing skin grafts or painful dressing changes or exhaustion from doing something so typically effortless for most of us, like talking or moving an inch. Watching my husband battle pain every day made me feel powerless. I wanted to do something, anything.

David

My initial stay at the hospital was a blur, not just mentally but physically. I wasn't able to wear my eyeglasses until a few weeks before I was discharged, so I couldn't see very well or very far. I knew there was a TV in the room because I could make out the borders of the dark, boxy appliance and hear the sound coming from it; I just couldn't see the picture. Whenever nurses or visitors would trail in and out of the room, I couldn't tell who was who until they got really close. Not being able to see well and drifting in and out of sleep didn't make for a comforting existence. I lost track of time quite easily, especially not being able to see the clock.

I remember early on, in the first week, being well aware of the heat lamps above me. Lying flat most of the time made me very familiar with the ceiling. The lamps glowed a bright orange and made me feel like I was under a gas broiler. Many times I wondered how long the doctors and nurses would leave me under those things until I'd be fully cooked.

I was back in the tub room about a week after I was admitted to the burn unit. Though I don't remember much of the tub room fiasco in my early stay, the following is based on what I do remember during my later visits there as well as Carly's journal and medical records. Also, visits to the tub room were frequent and for the most part consisted of the same treatments.

I remember a nurse once warning me that it was going to hurt. She just didn't say how badly. That particular day, for close to two hours, the dressings on my body were removed and the dead skin scrubbed off and cleaned. Half of the 2,000 staples from my grafting surgery were also removed. It took about four nurses to do this so I wouldn't have to spend any more time in the tub room than absolutely necessary. I was lying down on that cart, pain screaming its way through every inch of my body as my skin was picked clean of necrotic tissue and metal staples. Thankfully, I couldn't see the running trail of blood and chunks of dead skin left behind. I can't even begin to describe what it smelled like.

Receiving medication during the tub room procedure was an insolvable puzzle. Someone had once told me there wasn't enough pain medication to give burn patients, but obviously one needed to be drugged up on something. I found the more drugs I was given, the weirder the experience. Like a bad acid trip weird. For instance, there were times I believed the tub room was a literal means of punishment. I hadn't done something right that day so I was forced to be tortured. One time I was convinced the nurses were using the procedure to turn me into a ham and cheese sandwich, which was going to lead to my inevitable death. My heart would race and paranoia would set in, causing me to build more stress for the next tub room experience. On another occasion, I believed the nurses had stolen my hands and that after I got better, they'd give them back to me, looking pre-accident normal. I also remember one time as I lay on the shower table looking down and seeing my hip. I could make out the slits from the emergency escharotomies, except at the time, I didn't know the cuts were from a medical procedure. Instead, I thought doctors had moved my butt to my hip. As I was being scrubbed and cleaned and scraped, I stared at the ceiling in horror, wondering how I could ever again sit with a butt now positioned where my hip once was. Or better yet, how I would ever be able to go to the bathroom? I told you, a bad acid trip.

One time, after I was getting settled back into my room after a visit to the tub room, a nurse was trying to give me the magical dose of morphine to ease my pain. Unfortunately, the amount she gave me was more than I could handle and it caused me to stop breathing. Luckily, a doctor was also in my room and he began beating on my chest and throat. Carly watched in shock as the nurse flushed out my IV with a drug that counteracted with the powerful morphine and my body began to respond again. Administering the correct dose of pain medication is a tricky thing on a burn unit.

The combination of the excruciating pain and the mental trip to Crazyland built up an enormous amount of anxiety every time I was wheeled on a stainless steel cart to the tub room. It was maddening. I knew it to be a necessary evil, but it was nothing short of a ritual of agony.

After the debridement process, I was slathered with medicated burn cream, re-bandaged, and rolled back into my room. Immediately after, most times, I was out of it. Delirious. Physically exhausted from the intense pain. Sometimes still hallucinating. On numerous occasions, I'd return to my room suffering from septic shock, convulsing either because my body temperature was too high or too low. This happened when bacteria present on my body got stirred up during the cleaning and scrubbing process. The infection would move from the surface into my bloodstream and needed to be combatted with IV and topical antibiotics.

As an engineer, it was hard not to be in the driver's seat, not having any say in what happens when. I wanted to know when I'd need to be in the tub room next. I wanted some notice to mentally prepare myself as much as I could to try to keep my faculties in check. It was tough. I wouldn't wish the tub room, physically or psychologically, on my worst enemy.

Outside of being in that dreaded tub room, when I was present and not so doped up, I felt more in control. More myself, though I could feel the weight of disappointment begin to hound me. I was realizing, in bits and pieces, that my recovery process was slow. Really slow. Oh sure, I could talk. And I could move my head, wiggle my toes, and lift my arms and legs a little, but I was still stuck in a hospital, bandaged from head to toe. The short hospital stay I had anticipated just after getting licked by the flames during the accident was obviously a delusion. Realizing that put me in occasional funks.

Nurse Mary was always spreading her optimism around like some magic fairy dust. She encouraged me to repeat positive affirmations. "David," she would gently tell me. "Say, 'I am strong.'"

I'd look at her and whisper, "Mary is strong."

"No, no, no," she'd shake her head with a smile. "You say that *you* are strong."

"I am strong," I'd bounce back, adding, "And Mary is strong, too!"

Being able to talk to my wife, when I wasn't mumbling nonsense, was such a gift. Sometimes I couldn't do more than look at her, speak with my eyes and hope she'd figure out my cryptic gazes. Mostly, I wanted her to know that I loved her. And I hoped I got that across clear as day. I'm not proud to admit, but every now and then I'd get a little short with Carly. Especially during that first week when I would ask for a Sprite or Coke and she'd return with a Dixie cup full of ice chips or worse, Boost, a yucky, chalky nutritional drink. Talk about kicking a man when he's already down.

Carly

A day or two before David's second surgery on August 30th, I had the chance to spend most of the day with him, alone. Words, though slow and few, came easy to David as his level of alertness was increasing. I wrote this in my journal:

> *His gentle sarcasm and humor is still there. David is such a strong man! It's amazing that he still has a way of making me feel safe and strong when I'm with him.*

To this day, I am in awe of how not only my husband fought tirelessly for his life, but knowing he was confined to a bed, most of his body severely burned, he had a deep capacity for being funny, freckling what was still very much a veiled situation with optimism.

We still had a ton of support from friends and family. David's parents, Keith and Marilyn, and mine, Chuck and Rie, as well as David's sisters Amber, and Teresa, kept vigil in the hospital. Clyde and Linda, also regular staples when their schedules allowed, rented a few rooms for us at a motel across the street. There, we caught up on sleep or showered, and tag-teamed shifts so someone was with David at all times.

Having private time, being able to breathe without nurses, doctors, or family members near or around me was pacifying at times. Other times, it gave me space to think about what I didn't want to. Yes, the critical 48-72 hours had passed. Yes, David was for the most part breathing on his own. But the thought that the doctors hadn't given us a positive prognosis loomed overhead. Matter of fact, no one said anything remotely close to that until David was actually discharged four months later.

I used my solitude in the motel room to pray, to cry. And I did the same in the quiet hallways of the hospital, outside the BICU. I had given my heart to Christ in the early days of attending my hometown church in Minnesota. Years later, in another journey of spiritual awakening, I realized I needed to give my life to Him. But it wasn't until I was curled up on a hallway floor, praying and having my quiet time with the Lord, that I believe I fully surrendered every part of my being to Him. I didn't have a choice. I couldn't walk this journey on my own. I couldn't shoulder the fear of David dying. I couldn't bury myself under "what if" questions. I had to trust that our family was in God's hands and that He would take care of us. Because try as hard as I might, with all the good intentions, positive affirmations, willpower, and emotional coping mechanisms I could scrounge up, I just didn't know how. I love what Abraham Lincoln said, "I have been driven many times upon my knees by the overwhelming conviction that I had no where else to go. My own wisdom and that of all about me seemed insufficient for that day." Oh, how I relate.

David's second surgery, with more extensive debriding and grafting than the first, was scheduled for Monday, August 30th. Dr. Herndon, the hospital's chief of surgery and author of *Total Burn Care*, still to this day considered to be the bible of burn care, spoke to David's parents and me the day before surgery. A white-haired man of small stature and a big presence, Dr. Herndon was a nice guy, though sometimes gruff. He never minced his words and always told it like it was. That day he gave us sparse details about the surgery and said we should all hope for the best.

At 6 a.m. on the day of David's surgery, Jim, one of the nurses, tall and bald with dimples and a whitish-gray goatee, gently patted my shoulder to wake me up. I was in a dead sleep, exhausted from the lack thereof, slumped over on one of the vinyl couches in the family waiting room. David was talking, saying a lot of things that didn't make much sense to Jim.

Jolted awake, I rushed out of the waiting room, whipped on a gown and pair of gloves from the supply closet near the doorway, and rushed into David's room as he mumbled nonsensically.

"The master valve…"

"I was just waiting to reach for 108 pressure…"

"We're a team. We've just been playing til now…"

Then, he asked for Clyde.

While Clyde had been a valuable presence throughout this ordeal, he had been hesitant about talking to David. Praxair was still trying to piece together the details of the accident, and Clyde was worried anything he said about what had happened would upset David. He didn't talk to David that day, but the two of them did end up speaking about the accident a few days later. They talked about the moments right before the explosion and tried to think about if either of them had possibly done something to cause it or if their procedure had been wrong. They couldn't think of anything. Clyde told David that most of the evidence was destroyed in the fire. Praxair's best guess was that during construction something like grease had been inadvertently left in the new piping or a valve that caused it to ignite when it came into contact with the oxygen. More than likely the piping hadn't been cleaned properly for oxygen service.

Before David was wheeled into surgery an hour or two later, he reached out for my hand. A moment so brief, it was a simple brushing of the skin. And then he winked and was wheeled through the double doors of the operating room entrance. Little did I know that this would be the last time my husband and I would be able to have any physical contact for weeks.

Five hours later, Dr. Herndon, still scrubbed, came into the room as the nurses wheeled my husband back in.

"Surgery went beautifully," he said with confidence.

Because David had been battling infections from his first grafts, some of the initial graft locations on his arms and legs needed to be re-grafted with longer strips of new cadaver skin. His own skin, taken from his scalp, was used to regraft his thighs. Because his chest showed no signs of infection but rather evidence of potential healing on its own, doctors left that part of his body untouched. Also, because David was losing so much blood from these procedures, the operating room was stocked with twenty pints of blood. He only required nine. Lastly, his creatinine and glucose levels were beginning to drop to normal, his temperature was good, and his electrolytes were leveling—all good signs deserving of a big sigh of relief. At least momentarily, we could all stay grounded in the present.

During grafting procedures, doctors would be able to extract a bit of unburned skin from my husband's scalp, peeling it away with what looks shockingly similar to a cheese slicer. This skin, called autografts, was stretched out and placed over some of the burns. (And would hopefully stick permanently.) Amazingly, the scalp is quick to regenerate itself and this process could be repeated every seven to ten days.

It would take about seven days to assess each graft and determine whether or not placement was successful. If the site didn't turn black (necrotic) but stuck to his body, the nurses would use the term, "the graft has taken."

I sat with David after the surgery was over. Some parts of his body had been bandaged, but other parts were exposed. I noticed his scalp appeared to be bleeding, running with a rich red color. Frightened by what I thought was my husband's bleeding head, I called out for a nurse who rushed in to see what was wrong. "Oh, that's not blood," she assured me and explained that after doctors took skin from his scalp, they wrapped his head in gauze dipped in what's called Scarlet Red, a petroleum-based wound dressing that had a particularly disturbing color. I was thankful it wasn't evidence of a bleeding scalp, but boy it looked freaky.

A few days after surgery, I finally got to take a look at David without his bandages during his first dressing change. After the second round of grafting, Nurse Rachel, a tall, thin woman with a reassuring smile, gently began to unwrap a thick layer of Ace bandages around his neck, arms, and legs, and then the Polymyco dressings, a gauze infused with a yellow, antibiotic cream. My husband's bare body looked like a bloody patchwork quilt of bumpy, red and black scraps of skin held together with what looked like thousands of staples. You try not to be horrified when looking at something that's not supposed to look a certain way, but you can't help it. But it's not like I stood there gawking. I just repeated in my mind that David was alive and the rest, the reworking and rebuilding of skin, would come in time.

More surgery was scheduled that week. There were a few black spots and signs of infection on David's abdomen, as well as a few grafts that didn't stick and needed to be replaced. From this point on, my husband would have about a surgery a week.

David

Knowing that there was some deep-water oil rig construction going on in the Galveston Bay, (and thanks to the hallucinatory side effects of the pain meds) at times I believed the doctors had tasked me with underwater welding to earn my keep at the hospital. My breathing tube felt like an underwater breathing apparatus, the flickering light from a bad fluorescent bulb outside my room was the arc from the welding process, and the beeping of monitors mimicked the sound of the construction equipment. This feeling of being underwater stayed with me for years. After I finally got home, whenever I'd swim in a pool, I found comfort floating face down in the water for long periods of time. For some reason, doing this brought me a sense of peace, though I constantly had to endure screaming by lifeguards to turn face up.

My memory of what Carly called a "major milestone", as scribbled in her journal on Thursday, September 2, underlined and complete with stars, is fuzzy. But I do remember the gasps, the cheers, and the applause when I took my first steps that morning.

Movement was important. A mix of occupational and physical therapy began pretty quickly and ranged from positioning my body in the bed to promote healing, moving and stretching my limbs, to helping me sit up and get out of bed into a chair. Activity, however small, was crucial so my muscles wouldn't atrophy or my skin contract. When skin is burned and grafts placed, the surrounding skin begins to pull together, resulting in a contracture. If left untreated over a joint, this complication can restrict mobility and range of motion. Stretching out the skin and limbs, and sometimes even putting a splint over the joint, prevents this from happening. Movement and increasing range of motion is also critical to prevent heterotopic ossification, another complication of severe burns that involves the abnormal formation of extra bone.

That day, it took about eight people to sit me up and then get me standing. Then, with sixteen hands surrounding my bandaged and weak body, I shuffled lethargically a few steps forward toward a nearby recliner. I got winded with each step, unsure if I had the stamina necessary for the round trip journey. And while I could see hope glimmer in the eyes of Carly and my parents, everyone beaming and saying with great pride how they couldn't believe I was walking, all I could think was a defeated, "Walking? Oh no. This isn't walking. This is nothing even remotely close to walking."

On the plus side, once I was carefully seated in the recliner, my nurse, Rachel, asked what I wanted to drink as a reward for my gargantuan effort, "Apple juice?" she suggested with theatrical enthusiasm.

I shook my head and crinkled my nose as I sat back, taking slow and steady breaths. A vanilla milkshake was my drink of choice. A few minutes later, my request was granted. It was smooth down my throat, but warm—not an adjective you want used to describe a milkshake. I had a feeling the "milkshake", which was actually melted vanilla ice cream, was diluted with Boost. Turns out I was right. But hey, beggars can't be choosers, right?

I would need to get used to how different my life was going to be. These awakenings didn't happen at one juncture of epiphany, but in tiny spurts, here and there, as my lucidity allowed. I remember in those first few weeks hearing a lot of "Everything is going to be okay, David," which to me meant that everything was eventually going to be just like it was before the accident. That I would be able to work and run and fix things and bathe and brush my teeth and mow the lawn and repair appliances and be intimate with my wife just like I had prior to the accident. But that wasn't the case. "Everything is going to be okay," meant something entirely different. For starters, it was more of an encouragement that at the very least, I was going to live.

In the same vein, once I was able to sit up regularly and actually look at my skin grafts, which happened toward the end of my hospital stay, doctors would come in to see how the grafts were taking and remark, "Oh wow! That looks beautiful!" But again, at least to me, it didn't. My skin looked like a patchy, rough, discolored mess. The beauty, of course, lay in the fact that the grafts were doing what they were supposed to be doing, but it didn't match the vision in my head of what my skin should look like. My recovery was about perspective. And I would continue to learn this over the course of my stay in the BICU and in the years to come.

This new life, a life I was still in the throes of fighting for, was wrought with so many unknowns, it was impossible to process, let alone navigate. I didn't know what to expect. And I felt, like I'm sure Carly did many times, in the dark as to what was happening, what was going on with my skin, how many grafting procedures it was going to take to look normal, what I could expect to look forward to the next day or week. I begged Carly and the nurses soon after my second surgery for a schedule or something that would give me structure...anything, to piece together a plan. Of course, nobody could adequately accommodate my request. My situation was still critical and could change drastically for the worse at any moment. But they humored me and put up a dry erase board where I could see it without needing to strain my eyes. It listed a loose timetable of when I would eat and so forth. Even though the schedule changed often, it made me feel better and gave me a sense of control. And really, that was more or less the point.

Carly

When David walked for the first time, I was beside myself. I didn't care how long it took for him to shuffle one foot in front of the next. All that mattered was that he was moving. I was so proud of my husband and kept reminding him as he took step after step of how strong he was. I'm pretty sure in that moment all of us in the room, David's parents, the nurses and I jumped for joy—once our beloved patient was safe and secure in the recliner, of course—tears slipping down our cheeks. Frankly, anything David did, over and above wiggling his toes was progress, space to plant hope.

And I made sure he knew that, trying as best as I could to encourage him.

David was pretty talkative the rest of that particular day, though I'm not sure how much of our conversations, which were pretty scattered, he remembered. He asked a lot about his injuries.

"They don't tell me everything, Carly," David sighed.

"I know," I said, nodding. "Me either." He knew he was burned 94% of his body and that a slew of surgeries lay ahead, but that was about it.

"They should put duct tape on my skin," he suggested at one point that night. "It's a lot cheaper."

As night fell and the unit got quieter, the footsteps of visitors slowing to none, the company of doctors thinning out, David and I sat in silence for a while. The quiet was dotted by the hum and beeping of machines, a sound that had almost started to become melodic.

I looked at my husband and asked, "What are you thinking about, David?"

He didn't answer right away. And I'm not sure he even looked in my eyes when he finally spoke in a hushed tone, "Living through the next thing."

I nodded, reconnecting again to the prior silence. We were both thinking that very thing.

* * *

David's third surgery went well. Cadaver skin was still used during that procedure, but Dr. Sanford told us that the cultured skin would be ready and on its way from Boston in about two weeks. While David was relatively stable after surgery, and heavily sedated, Nurse Mary taught me how to care for the wounds on David's face. She soaked gauze in a solution of water and saline and laid it on his face for a few minutes to soften and loosen the dead skin and dried blood. Then I removed the now icky gauze and using Q-tips, removed the remaining gunk off his face. It wasn't the most glamorous of jobs, but I enjoyed it. It was something I could do to help my husband. A full two weeks hadn't yet passed since the accident, but I was growing very tired of being helpless, watching everyone work on him, except me.

The rest of the day, David dozed in and out of consciousness. At one point he looked at me, his eyes hazy and clouded. "Can you get me my dad's pocketknife?," he asked.

I looked at him, befuddled. "What are you talking about?"

"His pocketknife," David repeated. "Mine exploded."

I didn't realize until much later that the pocketknife he had always carried with him to work had disintegrated in the accident.

* * *

On Labor Day weekend, Clyde and Linda brought Samantha and Nathan down to spend some time with me. Unfortunately, it wasn't the warm and fuzzy reunion that I had hoped for. As the weekend progressed, I noticed the kids were getting sick, worse every few hours. Nathan looked pale and sickly and had developed a mean cough. Samantha was no better off. She complained of a sore throat and had nasal discharge. They were so sick, I didn't even dare venture anywhere near the hospital with the kids. We stayed put at the motel across the street.

I was a wreck, surrounded by my two ill children, but quickly slapped on my mom-mode hat, lending them some overdue cuddles at the motel, before heading back to the hospital again. As it was, any time I headed down to the cafeteria for some water or to the motel for a quick shower or power nap, I felt a growing anxiety. *What would I miss? What if David took a turn for the worse?* The guilt of leaving my husband even for a few minutes felt like an anvil bearing down on my chest. But here I was, feeling the same kind of crushing guilt, as I cradled now-feverish Nathan in my arms and wiped miserable Samantha's gunky nose.

Thankfully, my mom and dad agreed to step in and took the kids to the emergency room in the adjacent children's hospital. An hour or two later, my parents got in touch with me. Sam had a bad sinus infection and was given antibiotics and went back to the motel with my mother. Nathan wasn't so lucky. Doctors suspected pneumonia and recommended he stay overnight.

Now I had no choice but to leave David's side. I had to get to the children's hospital and be with Nathan. My saving grace was that Keith and Marilyn, David's parents, and his sister, Teresa, were able to stay with my husband. While that gave me some relief, I had to contend with a sick child in an emergency room I hadn't a clue how to get to. For Pete's sake, I could barely find my way to the BICU when David was admitted.

Teresa had been to the children's hospital earlier that week with her infant daughter, Abbie and knew how to navigate her way around the campus. With her as a more than capable guide and dear friend, we shuttled through the maze-like walkways and underground corridors.

Walk Through Fire

After successfully leading me to the emergency room, Teresa hugged me goodbye as she left to return to David's bedside. I hurried through the slew of paperwork waiting at the admissions desk, and then finally, I was able to hold Nathan. He lay on my chest, lethargic and burning with fever. My heart ached for him as he squirmed and whimpered in pain when the nurse inserted a catheter to take a urine sample and started an IV for fluid intake. I felt broken, wondering how much more our family could possibly take. Oh sure, I'd heard the annoying platitude that God would never give anyone more than they could handle, but give me a break!

It's hard to explain what happened next, but I had a strong sense overpower me that the enemy/Satan was attacking our family. I felt battered in the midst of a spiritual war with unseen forces. Biting back tears as I rubbed my baby boy's back, I whispered out loud to the darkness, "You are not going to win."

My dad and I spent the night in the children's hospital. I held Nathan in the rocking chair so he wouldn't be forced to sleep in the hospital steel cage crib. I was relieved to sign the discharge papers early the next morning, but sad to the see the kids go back home to Nederland with their grandparents. At 9:30 that morning, I finally went back to the motel across the street to get some rest.

I lay in bed, unable to sleep for a long time. Though I was so grateful for our friends from church taking turns watching the kids, taking Samantha to school, helping her with her homework, and making sure she and Nathan kept a somewhat regular routine, I wasn't sure if a constant change of hands was in their best interest. They needed more balance, a normal that I couldn't give them quite yet. The next day I asked my father if he would stay with the kids at our home in Nederland until David was discharged. I knew my Dad would be overwhelmed at first. He'd been retired for years and hadn't ever watched multiple kids all day, but I also knew how much he despised hospitals. I had a feeling handling the challenge of a spirited toddler and feisty nine-year-old was a whole heck of a lot better than sitting around an antiseptic smelling sanatorium where the smell of death lingered, softly but always present. I was right. My father bravely accepted the task.

5.

David

Boost.

Just writing the word makes me want to vomit. The nutritional supplement drink, chock-full of vitamins and minerals, made me gag every time anyone stood over me, holding a can of that unholy drink, a pastel-colored straw angled menacingly in my direction.

"Drink up!" they'd say, as if giving me the lost ark of nutrition.

Despite my wide-eyed looks of horror and the stomach churning that would always begin once I saw the can of Boost heading my way, I had to slurp it down as best as I could. I had no choice.

It wasn't long after my accident that doctors encouraged me to start eating and drinking. While I wasn't chomping on filet mignon or lobster tails right away, it was important for me consume 3,500 or more calories a day. Because my body had been through so much trauma and I had lost a lot of weight, it was basically feeding on my muscle tissues. To prevent my body from turning into a useless machine, I had to eat like a sumo wrestler or a marathoner. For the first two plus months, I had a feeding tube, which would pump nutrition into my body. In addition, I had to ingest cans and cans upon cans of Boost.

But even though they carried a can or two of the dreaded nutritional drink with them, I was grateful when the ones I loved visited with me hour after hour, praying with and talking to me. Though I don't remember every person who walked in, or would forget who came the following day, I have a general sense of the sea of familiar faces. Carly, my cheerleader, was always there with a smile on her face. My parents were rocks, steady and sure, reminding me of their love and God's faithfulness. My sisters, Teresa and Amber, too, stood with me off and on those first two or three weeks, chatting away as girls often do, light twinkling in their eyes. There was my college buddy Rob, our friends Jackie, Helene, Gordon, the list goes on and on. It was an incredible feeling being enveloped by this patchwork of love and support.

And, last but not least, Clyde, my friend and mentor, joined this lengthy vigil with me proving once again his compassionate and committed character. A few weeks after my admission, he brought in a boom box with some books on tape. The gesture was awesome, and helped pass some of my downtime alone outside of listening to whatever was on the TV. But when Clyde brought with him *Executive Order*, Tom Clancy's political and military thriller novel, I started hallucinating hours after the nurse had stopped playing the tape. I was adamant monkeys carrying the deadly Ebola virus were making their way into the U.S. Sometimes my paranoia would get the best of me, and I would, with great passion and conviction, make outlandish claims. Whether it was Carly or my parents who were beside me, I'd talk gibberish about the threat of biological warfare.

But whoever was listening to me at the time would remain patient and simply listen. Mom would often tell me later, "David, my goodness! There were so many times you were talking and you'd just run way out into left field. And we'd have to try and slowly bring you back." I felt better, however, knowing there were equal times when I was coherent and made sense, even though the next day I would occasionally forget what was said.

There were many times lying in that hospital bed, when I could see past the wounds, past the bandages, past the collage of family photographs Carly had posted on a wall parallel to my bed, past the nurses, and out the glass door of my room. It was a mental vision, picturing what Carly was doing, what she was going through. I'm sure Carly was either hounding doctors with more questions, hanging out in the waiting room with the growing number of visitors from work, church and our community, or schlepping back and forth from the motel to the hospital after getting some much-needed sleep. I worried about her. I couldn't even begin to understand the weight of change and shifting responsibilities she had to take in and accommodate in the last two weeks.

Everything was different. This wasn't an easy road for any of us, but my heart was heavy knowing that while all I had to focus on was my recovery, she had to care for me, for the kids, for the house, and herself. What a feat. All I could do was pray that God would surround her with a strength only He could give, a strength that would help take her from day to day without falling apart.

Carly

Another dance of joy was in store when two weeks after the accident, David ate his first actual meal. His sister Teresa sat by his side, dipping a plastic fork into a plateful of buttery tetrazzini. It wasn't bad, but tasted nothing like David's mother's delicious and much requested recipe. Teresa lovingly fed him, slow bite by slow bite. By the time he announced he was full, in addition to most of the pasta, he had gulped down three cartons of milk as well as a dinner roll. David's nutritionist had made clear to us that he needed to eat high calorie foods, and we needed to keep meticulous records of every bite he took to ensure we were all following orders.

It was a glutton's paradise. The meals came fast and furious. Some the hospital provided, others my in-laws, Keith and Marilyn, would bring in from their lunches or dinners at local restaurants. Not surprisingly, hospital food wasn't very tasty and because the kitchen was on a seven-day rotation, meal options were limited. We would sit by David's side, cut a piece of fish or pasta and dip it deep into a canister of melted butter, adding as much caloric weight as we could, and feed him to his heart's content. Some days he was hungrier than others. For the most part, David enjoyed the food.

To me, the milestones were adding up to many. These were markers that helped me plod along this emotionally tiring road of destination unknown. I needed to relish in every milestone that came our way, because doctors were performing the same song and dance. They cautioned us that though David was staying the course, things could change for the worse rather quickly.

Every time the team of residents or attendings made their rounds or popped their heads in to check on David's progress, they marveled at the fact that my husband had survived this far. Sadly, most patients burned as severely as David did not. But their smiles and nods of hope were always short-lived. "Let's wait and see how David fares," was the Cliff Notes answer to my question of how he was doing.

While I counted on them for their medical expertise and experience, I relied heavily on the nurses, wonderful, knowledgeable men and women like Rachel, Mary, Verna, and Jamie during the day and Jim or Basil during the evening. Many of them smoked, given the high level of stress. Burn unit nurses work in an environment that is particularly challenging physically and emotionally. Patients with severe burns have some of the most horrific injuries and agonizingly painful recoveries. A lot of the medically necessary procedures, like the dreaded cleaning/debridement in the tub room, cause excruciating pain for the burn survivor. This leads to a very emotional experience for those taking care of them, especially the nurses. These medical workers also have to deal with the high mortality rate of severely burned patients, I found that those who are unable to handle the emotions detach. While I understand this to be a common coping mechanism, it leads to a less compassionate service for the patient. But for the most part, the nurses who treated David were incredible, steadfast in their tenderness. These men and women would take their smoke breaks outside, pulling me along for the walk so I could enjoy fifteen minutes here and there with the sunlight basking on me and the fresh salty air refreshing my lungs.

I'd pepper them with questions about David, his grafts, his surgeries, his stats. But I wouldn't always just ask them medical queries. I wanted to know, in their experience, how life would look if he left the BICU alive. I grew especially close to Rachel and Verna and hounded them with question after question. What kind of physical limitations would David live with? Would he be able to work again? Would we be able to have more children? They were warm and supportive as well as cautiously optimistic and realistic. They would answer my questions as time progressed and it was clear my husband would survive.

The outpouring of support from the Team David community continued. A DBU dated September 6, 1999, recorded that people in twenty-two states and four countries were praying for our family. Blood drives were being coordinated where family members, friends, and even complete strangers donated. A woman from our church sent us multiple single containers of soup, banana pudding, and other comfort foods packed in coolers. Many folks helped out my dad back home. Though he was doing a wonderful job caring for Samantha and Nathan to the best of his ability, there was always an extra body or two around to pitch in. A woman from our church would pick up my daughter from school a few times a week to do her hair and help with homework.

Other friends brought meals on a regular basis so my father didn't have to suffer only eating boxed mac and cheese and chicken nuggets. During this time, Gordon would say that these people who loved on, prayed for, and supported us during this experience were the pictorial definition of the Church, the way followers of Christ are created to love and serve others. He's right.

In addition to the family photos I had tacked on the wall in David's room, I had posted a slew of get-well cards. Thousands came in over the course of his hospital stay from kids at Samantha's school, well-wishing strangers around the world, and our friends from home and church. I can't tell you how much they brightened the drab décor of David's room, where most of the color came from the bold or printed scrubs the nurses would wear.

Marilyn Myers, administrator of the DBUs, continued to send out updates to the Team David community, sometimes daily, other times weekly, most times staying up way past the midnight hour to write and send out the emails. Because I didn't have access to the internet at the hospital, she would print and send to the hospital some of the emails she received in reply, which reinforced to me the existing and growing prayer circle that surrounded our family. With these prayers, support, encouragement, and kindness, our family was able to stay strong. We will never be able to express our appreciation and thanks.

David

The day after I ate my first meal, it was time for another tub room visit. These were pretty frequent events unless I had a surgery, which afforded me about a week break from the dreaded torture chamber. While I barely remember this particular tub room visit, I had plenty of lucid moments there. James, one of the nurses, liked to talk while working on me. Though he had a heavy accent and his voice was somewhat muffled because he had to wear a mask, I liked talking to the guy. He always played music, particularly the Beatles, a helpful diversion, asked a lot of questions, and shared an equal amount about himself, his passions and hobbies, particularly carpentry. James was a fun, optimistic character with a big personality. I have fond memories of the guy except for the time he had to remove a staple in my scrotum from a graft. It was beyond excruciating, though he kept assuring me he was being as gentle as possible.

If I ever had a nurse who wasn't as chatty or friendly working on me in the tub room, I'd do math in my head to help distract me. The shower table doubled as a weight scale. I'd compare my current weight in kilograms with the previous day's tub room visit and spend a few minutes converting the difference into pounds. Another helpful diversion.

What I do remember that particular day was what happened afterward. I hadn't been sleeping well, unable to settle into a deep rest for more than a few minutes at a time during the night. That, coupled with the high dosage of pain meds I was given right before nurses furiously scrubbed my skin clean put me in a delirious state. All I wanted to do after spending hours in the tub room was to lie down in bed and shut the world around me off for a little while. It wasn't an option. On the contrary, nurses informed me it was time to get up and get moving. With muddied mental faculties, I can recall this best with the help of Carly's journal.

Sporting fresh bandages on top of freshly scraped skin, with much of my strength dependent on the two or three nurses encircling me, I shuffled over to a cardiac chair, a re-engineered and well-cushioned recliner with multiple configurations. Then, I was wheeled out of the burn unit for the first time. Carly and my mom flanked my sides, asking me questions about how I was doing, words I heard as if they came from a far distance. I don't remember much of the scenery I passed on my way out. For the most part the walls, dotted with soothing artwork, and doorways, rolled past in a haze.

The farther I was wheeled, the brighter the backdrop. For forty-five minutes, I sat upright in a hospital hallway that connected to a skywalk spanning the street below. Windows lined the length of the hallway wall, opening up the long and wide corridor to the warm glow of the sun. I dozed on and off during that time, my sight dimmed from fatigue. I vaguely remember the chatter of my mother and Carly talking to the nurses about medical procedures or asking me what I thought of the view, a small, empty playground area and the Shriner's Hospital across the way. While the scenery wasn't as breathtaking as staring at a painting by Monet, it was comforting. It offered the familiar trappings of a world that keeps on moving, even when you can't.

As I started gaining more lucidity, Carly asked if I wanted to sit in the family waiting room for a bit, another change of scenery. Some of the kids from youth group, including Ashley and Big Nate, were visiting and wanted so badly to see me.

I nodded. "Of course."

There's just something about young people that brings a palpable energy to a room. When I was wheeled in, I think a part of me expected to see uncomfortable looks on their faces, or eyes wide at the sight of their former youth leader bandaged like a mummy except for his red and raw face. No such thing. They were a barrel of laughs, a pack of loud and rambunctious comedians. They even came bearing a gift.

"Look at what we found in the middle of the road on the way here," Big Nate blurted out, proudly holding a bowling ball up to his chest and struggling with the weight.

Carly and I couldn't help but laugh. "Take care of it for me," I told them, trying to keep a straight face.

I was sad to see them go, to watch as their smiles, their jokes, and their playfulness trailed out of the room one by one. I missed the youth group kids. And seeing them made that wound ache even more. By the time I was wheeled back in my room and the nurses and Carly painstakingly helped me back in bed, I was a wreck. I felt out of it again, paranoia taking the place of what had been a relatively peaceful past few minutes. Agitated, I couldn't stand being in my own skin, literally and figuratively. It wasn't long before my blood pressure skyrocketed and my breathing became unstable. As I lay gasping for air, I could make out the fear on Carly's face, as well as my parents, as nurses pumped more medicine through my IVs and pressed buttons on the beeping machines. I ended up mellowing out an hour or so later, but it was evidence of how my mind and my body vacillated from one minute to the next. I'd say I looked forward to sleeping, but knowing I hadn't slept well in a few days, I didn't hold much hope.

Carly

A little more than two weeks after the accident, David was a lot more mobile, getting wheeled in this monstrous cardiac chair where he could sit upright for a long period of time and even walking a bit, sometimes from bed to chair, other times a few feet more. "The more David moves, the faster his recovery," doctors continually quipped. Physical and occupational therapists showed up every day helping him increase his range of motion by stretching and bending his ankles, legs, arms, and fingers. And though almost every stint of intense movement prompted a look of disappointment in David's eyes that he wasn't moving as fast or as far as he would have liked, I was proud as a peacock.

After David's next, and fourth, surgery, we were told his cultured skin would arrive soon. I wasn't always well informed of David's surgical plan throughout his entire hospital stay. Many times that meant being told the day before that he'd need another surgery. And doctors wouldn't know what to expect or the details of the procedure until they were at work on David's body on the operating table.

Most of the pre-surgical information we got came from the helpful nurses. Through them we learned that David's fifth surgery would consist of grafting using the cultured skin. It would arrive at the hospital in four climate-controlled boxes, accompanied by a special medical carrier, each box assigned its own seat on a commercial flight. Each box held forty-eight 3" x 5" sheets of skin. Picture fifteen floor tiles. I marveled at medical science. I couldn't believe it was even possible for all of this cultured skin to be created from a mere postage-stamp size piece of real skin. It felt like we were in the middle of a science fiction movie.

* * *

I was now staying at a furnished condo a fifteen-minute drive away from the hospital. I don't even remember researching places. I'm pretty sure Clyde took care of this for me, making sure to find a place with a nice view and a pool. Same thing with my car. By this point, it was in Galveston but I don't know who brought it down for me. Funny how you forget little details.

Samantha and Nathan came down regularly and deserved a reprieve from the repressive and stodgy hospital environment. It didn't require much to keep them entertained; splashing around a pool was just fine. While Samantha visited David on occasion, Nathan still had not. David and I weren't sure it was such a good idea. He was only two and his father's appearance was more scary than welcoming for a toddler. We figured the time would eventually come to reunite, we just didn't know when.

While David was being fed and slowly munched on scrambled eggs, fresh fruit, mashed potatoes, apple pie, you name it (oh, and, of course, the required daily dosing of Boost), he wasn't doing so great in the sleep department.

I hated coming back to the hospital early in the morning and hearing another report from the nurses that he hadn't slept well. It seemed when he had those rough nights, he was quieter the next day—less talkative, more confused. I knew the marriage of the pain medication and the continuous physical toll on his body was affecting his sleep patterns for the worse. I also knew that this was to be expected because of the severity of his injuries. Still, it was disheartening. Not getting enough rest wasn't a good thing for his recovery.

It was a lot easier to be strong, to stay grounded and fixed in hope, when David was lucid, joking with me and the nurses, making his signature verbal jabs. When he wasn't, I had to make a choice. I had to choose joy in that moment. It was tempting sometimes to slink into despair, to allow the haunting questions that constantly churned in my brain, sometimes in whispers and other times in deafening lament, to overwhelm me.

Is David really going to be okay?

And what does okay mean?

Is he just one surgery away from taking a turn for the worse?

Do my kids hate me for not being around?

Are they even capable of understanding what's happening?

One of the verses in the Bible I often thought of during this time was Romans 15:13, "May the God of hope fill you with all joy and peace as you trust in Him, so that you may overflow with hope" (NIV). I began to understand the difference, the big difference, between joy and happiness. The two words are often confused or used interchangeably. Happiness is circumstantial. It can change depending on what you are going through or what you have in the moment. Many times we believe we will be truly happy when we get married, land that job, win the lottery, lose the weight, or when the kids are out of the house. Happiness is fleeting and typically evaporates in times of crisis.

Joy, on the contrary, is not dependent on circumstances. It's an attitude that requires courage, commitment, and strength. Deciding to live with joy, even seeking it out when we need to, allows us to face tough times head on. And not just to merely survive the experience, but to be shaped in an incredible way that changes us for good for life.

Many things helped me choose joy on a daily and even hourly basis. Sheila, a dear friend, had bought me a copy of Tim Hansel's book *You Gotta Keep Dancing*. She had never read it, but just happened to be in a bookstore one day when her eyes landed on the cover. Something stirred in her heart. She felt nudged by God to purchase the book for us.

Hansel, who passed away in 2009, wrote about discovering the true meaning of joy while suffering a lifetime of chronic panic, the result of a tragic mountain climbing accident in the Sierras. I read the book cover to cover in one sitting, sometime in the first few weeks of David's admission to the BICU. One thing Hansel wrote that struck me was, "Pain is inevitable but misery is optional. We cannot avoid pain, but we can avoid joy." [8] If we choose to ignore joy, we allow ourselves to be as miserable as we want to be. And while there might be something familiar or comforting digging our heels into that wretched place, there is another option—joy.

I had to learn to choose joy. It didn't come naturally most of the time. It wasn't an organic response when David was unconscious for the first forty-eight hours and doctors seemed pretty skeptical that he would survive. I had to consciously and intentionally choose joy when every part of my being wanted to crawl deep in a hole and stay there. I had to choose joy when my husband was in so much pain that taking as little as two steps left him barely able to breathe. I had to choose joy when my kids were sick, or missing their parents, or questioning what was happening. I found the more I chose to battle the urge to wallow in misery, the more habitual it became.

Being a witness to the kindness of those we knew and loved and others we'd never met before helped joy find a steady place in my heart. I'll never forget receiving an envelope in the mail one day while I was at the hospital that contained a letter and a check for twenty dollars. A woman I didn't know wrote heartfelt words of how she was a telemarketer and had called our home in Nederland to see if we were interested in some product or service. My father, Chuck, had answered the phone and a gabfest between them ensued. I have a feeling my dad, who probably hadn't had adult conversation all day, had talked her ear off, grateful for the exchange of phrases other than "Stop doing that", "Finish your dinner," and "Did you do your homework?" Through the conversation, this woman learned of David's accident and wanted to write us, wish us well, and send us whatever little money she could afford. Imagine that! A telemarketer offering us support!

It was little things like this that helped propel me forward and continue to choose joy, even when it wasn't easy. It wasn't long before I realized the strength I felt in my heart had nothing to do with my innate character. I wasn't this super human being who could waltz around the BICU spouting off trite clichés about staying positive. My ever-changing attitude of hope and joy was being formed, ever so slowly, by God himself. I love what Tim Hansel wrote, "The disillusionment with our own abilities is, perhaps, one of the most important things that can ever happen to us." It's another way of saying, "I can do all this through Christ who gives me strength" (Philippians 4:13, NLT) and, like the prophet Nehemiah wrote in Scripture, "The joy of the Lord is your strength" (Nehemiah 8:10, NIV).

I needed this supernatural strength every day, and especially for David's fifth surgery, where doctors would attempt to graft his body with the cultured skin. There was a lot of preparation before the big day, mainly taking off the bandages, cleaning the skin, and rewrapping everything in fine gauze, a dressing the nurses and I had affectionately come to call the " bridal veil." The cleaning process, as you know by now, is pretty extensive. And sometimes not just dead skin and tissue come off.

Prior to surgery, David was energetic and lucid during some parts of the day, lethargic and slurring his words during others. All in all, I never ceased being in awe of David's strength and fortitude. I wrote this in my journal on September 12, 1999:

> *Your (David's) strength amazes me, physical, mental, and spiritual. It's amazing that when I'm feeling a bit discouraged, I can go into your room and you have a way of making me feel better. Even in your condition, you are amazingly strong. I love you....It's so wonderful to talk with you. The first few days/week we were here, all you were able to do was wiggle your toes and blink those beautiful crystal blue eyes at me—that was a wonderful gift. But now we can talk to each other like there's no tomorrow and I savor ever minute.*

A day before the surgery, Rachel, David's main nurse who was quiet and very proficient, noticed his ear was all black and crusty, she whipped out a pair of scissors from her medical tool belt and trimmed it off and dropped it in the trash can. I had been warned earlier that this was a possibility because his ear was turning black. You'd think David losing an ear would be a traumatic event, but it didn't faze me. I just wanted David to live and trusted the nurses and doctors to do their job.

When the day finally came, I was excited, even though I carried a certain level of apprehension, as I did every time that David was wheeled into the operating room. Rachel walked with us down the long corridor that led to the surgery unit. As we walked back into the BICU, after I told David that I loved him and to behave, I noticed that Rachel, who had grown very attached to her patient, had tears in her eyes.

Gently clasping her shoulder I asked, "What's wrong, Rachel?"

"I just want to be able to fix David, that's all. He's been through so much," she told me, as a dam of tears built up behind her clear-rimmed glasses.

Five hours into surgery, Rachel swung by the waiting room with an update. A big smile rounded out her thin, oval face. "All the new skin is on and David is getting wrapped up with the bridal veil. He was stable throughout the surgery." Rachel beamed and gave us a thumbs-up sign, "So far so good!" All of us in the waiting room let out a big sigh, uttering words of praise to God. *So far so good is right!*

An hour later, David was wheeled back into his room. At first, doctors were skeptical that there would be enough cultured skin to cover David's entire body. They ended up having more than enough. His arms, legs, abdomen and chest were covered, as well as part of his neck and right side of his face. His own skin was taken from his scalp and placed on his underarm area. No grafts were needed on his back as it looked like it was healing properly. During surgery, doctors needed to amputate the tips of his fingers because of the amount of dead tissue present. Necrotic skin posed a great risk to patients because of the likely spread of life-threatening infection. So the rule of thumb in the operating room was "life over limb." If a patient's survival depended on amputating part or parts of a body, the decision was always to choose life.

The cultured skin was extremely thin, only a few cells thick, and very fragile. It was clear and looked wet, like a layer of watery mucous. To prevent the risk of losing these new skin cells and to enforce the no-contact rule, doctors fitted David into a complex traction device so the only thing touching his bed for the next six weeks would be his back. This scary looking contraption consisted of a system of aluminum poles, pulleys, ropes, and weights keeping his arms and legs elevated. Most of his joints were pinned to this device. His arms were bent in a 90-degree angle with each finger individually pinned in hopes of providing David with partial use of those digits. While it was common for burn patients receiving cultured skin grafts to use this device, it was rare for so much of it to be used at once. Some of David's physical and occupational therapists would bring in students to take a look at this anomaly. The one plus to the traction device was that it kept David out of the tub room for close to six weeks. All wound care was performed during that time in his room.

When I saw David for the first time after surgery, I admit, it was a bit alarming. The traction device looked like a maze of thin steel pins and wires jutting from his hands, arms and legs and six-inch-long pins covered in gauze were sticking out of his ankles and knees. It just looked painful and uncomfortable. But the threatening looking post-surgery visual didn't shadow my sense of relief and excitement at being by my husband's side.

"How did things go?" he asked me, sounding tired but surprisingly alert.

"It couldn't have gone better," I smiled.

"Do my legs look as good as my arms?"

I laughed. "You bet they do, honey!" Overwhelmed with joy, I wanted to kiss him so badly, but I knew I couldn't. Up until this point, any form of physical touch was off-limits, mainly to prevent infection. So imagine my surprise when Rachel, standing on the other side of the bed, piped up. "You know, Carly, I think David deserves a big kiss right here," she said, pointing to his forehead.

My heart leapt. I couldn't believe I was going to finally get to kiss my husband for the first time in over three weeks. I leaned in for the big smooch and even though a plastic oxygen mask covered most of David's face, I heard him kiss back. My knees were weak and shaking. It felt like a first kiss. And I was the typical giddy schoolgirl, about to run out of the room and down the hall of the BICU screaming at the top of my lungs that I kissed David Bowers! I remember writing in my journal that night, still feeling the rush.

We take so much for granted! After years of

marriage, we start feeling like we don't do as much for each other—the love notes, flowers, etc., aren't as frequent as they were when we were dating. It's not until now I realize how many little things everyday that we still did do. Touch is so important! I'm telling people to hug their spouses more, hold hands more, talk more, just enjoy life more!

I love you so much, David. I knew you were an incredible man before I married you, but through this I'm realizing how incredible you truly are.

God is holding us in the palm of His hand. Because I sure don't know where I'm getting my strength. This isn't something I would normally be able to handle. God is with us.

Before I left David that night and headed to the condo, we spent time watching a VHS tape that some friends from our former church in Minnesota had sent us. They shared a time of prayer and told some fun filled memories they had of David and me from our youth group days at Hastings UMC. They closed the video with a slightly off-key rendition of the song, "Our God is an Awesome God."

Moonlight peeked through the thin aluminum blinds covering the room's one window. The holy presence of the Divine was palpable, filling us with a sweet presence. In unison, David and I repeated, "God is good, all the time. All the time, God is good."

And before my husband drifted off to what I hoped would be a peaceful and long sleep, he sang softly, "An awesome God."

So true David, so true.

6.

David

"You stink," my wife gagged theatrically one late September morning while one of the nurses changing my bandages stifled a gasp.

How else could I respond but smile?

Carly wasn't trying to be mean or anything. Besides, she was right. I did smell pretty bad. But the problem wasn't a lack of good hygiene habits. I was as clean as you could get with a body that was 94% burned. The problem was that a strong bacteria, resistant to most antibiotics, was growing on my grafts. One of the doctors said that though he was concerned, he felt hopeful the infection would eventually go away. But in the meantime, I got regularly sprayed with Dakin's solution, a powerful antiseptic made from chlorine that's so strong it kills most forms of bacteria and viruses, even good skin cells. It also helps eliminate odors. Doctors, of course, would continue to monitor the infection to make sure it didn't get worse.

As my BICU stay progressed, I tried to keep my humor intact, especially with the nurses who would cycle in and out of my hospital room, checking my vitals, changing my bandages, spraying me with bacteria-be-gone. A burn unit isn't naturally a wellspring of smiles, giggles, and cheer. It's like the opposite of walking into the maternity nursery ward, where healthy and chubby babies automatically illicit streams of "oohs" and "ahhs." Yeah, not so much of that was happening in the BICU except for some doctors who would give me a thumbs-up sign on a graft that took well (big whoop!). So I had to get on with my sarcastic self. I may not have been much to look at all gauzed up, but at least I could muster some wit to lighten the monotonous, long, and painful days.

Being in the traction device—my extremities hanging in the air with pulleys, ropes, and pins—was demoralizing, not to mention uncomfortable. It was almost impossible to sleep without potent sleep meds. Whenever a nurse would walk in and ask me how I was doing, my answer was the same.

"Oh, just hanging around." Because that's basically all I did for a few weeks, my legs and arms suspended in the air like a Cirque du Soleil dancer.

The nurses would always talk amongst themselves while tending to my care. During the times I was fully awake, I tried to tune out personal talk so I wouldn't appear to be nosy or eavesdropping. But who are we kidding? I had nothing better to do than hang out and take in friendly gossip or casual chitchat. I remember one time someone was complaining about how hot it was outside. Granted, living in the Lone Star state was like living in the devil's armpit. Many Texans would say things like, "It's hotter out there than a billy goat in a pepper patch." When I heard one nurse grumble about the sweltering temperatures, I playfully chided her.

"Make sure you wear sunscreen. You don't want to get burned out there," I said, with a knowing nod.

But I wasn't always smiles and jokes. Every now and again, during the more lucid times, my mind reeled in thought. Discouragement set in. It happened more easily when my room was absent of loved ones, visitors, nurses, doctors. Those down times were supposed to promote rest, sleep. But many times the quiet and the unmistakable décor of a hospital room provided just the right breeding ground for my mind to spin in all sorts of crazy directions.

I began to struggle with the "why" question. And though at times I could temporarily placate the disturbing query, it haunted me. I struggled with the fact that I willingly went into work on my day off. I struggled with not knowing what caused the explosion. There were times I replayed the day in my head over and over, trying to see if I missed a detail or something that would help to answer the question. I struggled with knowing the accident and my injuries forced my wife to put her life on hold. I struggled with worry, thinking about our kids, living their new day-to-day lives, two and a half hours away from their mom and dad, a father who couldn't perform the most basic of life skills like feed himself or walk a few steps unassisted. I struggled not knowing if I would ever work again or, more importantly, be the same dad that I was before, one Samantha and Nathan deserved.

Why, God, why?

Early on, I was slowly coming to the conclusion that God was punishing me for something I had done or perhaps had not done. I had concocted an image of the Old Testament God, a God who was erratic, easily angered, and vindictive at the slightest provocation. The kind of God who does not have a sliding scale of grace, but exacted a certain punishment to fit a certain crime. And that it was this God, this false picture of the actual loving creator, who was making not only me, but my entire family pay for something. While I questioned God's reasons—which I still don't and may never know until I see Him face to face—I felt I needed to hold on to my faith, moment by moment. That I couldn't continue to view Him as cruel, a Deity who delights in the suffering of others.

The questioning would come and go, things Carly and I would process together more and more down the road. I've come to learn that it takes a big God to be able to handle our questions, our doubts, our ramblings, our wonderings. And I can't help but feel the very things that darkness hopes will drive a wedge between God and us are the same things that light purposes to draw us closer to Him.

My sister Teresa tells me how on one shift, the nurses were understaffed and needed some help to change my bedding. It was humbling, not being able to pitch in and simply do something. Teresa volunteered to help, quickly noticing my bummed expression. While she didn't offer trite suggestions to cheer me up, saying something like "Oh, David, just be grateful you have clean sheets," she did bring to mind the passage of Scripture she had been meditating on. It was powerful stuff.

My sister and the nurses carefully rolled me to my side,

a challenging feat in light of the traction device. Then they stripped the bed of dirty sheets and with military precision redressed it with new crisp white new ones—all the while Teresa repeated in a soothing voice, over and over,

"For we know that if the earthly tent we live in is destroyed, we have a building from God, an eternal house in heaven, not built by human hands." (2 Corinthians 5:1, NIV)

I watched and I listened, Teresa tells me, soaking in the words of the Apostle Paul. My earthly tent, my body, was all but destroyed. And while the thought of one day moving into an eternal house in heaven wasn't necessarily the most consoling thought at the time, it was a reminder that our tents, our earthly bodies, our homes, are temporary, not promised in fullness, but capable of disappearing, changing, or crumbling at any time. The eternal, our spirits, our relationship with God, is what matters.

My sister said that however annoyed I seemed at first, my temperament softened considerably by the time they were finished. I have a feeling I may have relaxed and drifted off into a long and deep sleep.

Carly

David was always asking how he looked. As a matter of fact, during one of Gordon's visits, he asked David what he'd like him to pray for. "The way I look," David responded. Without his glasses, he couldn't see very well, let alone visually grasp what his new skin looked like. Gordon and I, as well as David's parents and the nurses, repeatedly reassured him that he looked great. His face especially was healing well.

While David's skin wasn't as smooth as a baby's bottom, the fact was it was healing. And most of all, he was alive.

Though David would never look the same as he had prior to the accident and there wasn't much that could be done about it, other things were fixable. Like loosening his facial skin and muscles, which were so tight it hurt David to even smile. My husband's daily homework assignment was to close his eyes and scrunch up his face ten times consecutively several times a day as well as to recite the alphabet slowly and deliberately. Doesn't sound like much of a challenging assignment for an engineer like my husband, but it was a necessary part of his recovery. And these silly-looking exercises actually worked!

Another part of his recovery consisted of moving his feet. This meant me, still needing to wear gloves to prevent infection, standing at the foot of his bed and placing my hand on his toes as he pushed on my hand. Slow and steady progress, little movements over time. One day David moved his right leg a bit. Another time, he started moving his right arm up and down while in the traction device.

Aside from the continual progress, which included surviving surgeries, healing skin grafts, talking, and moving a little more each day, one piece of evidence of David's recovery that I savored was his laughter. Yeah, it hurt to smile because his skin was stretched so taut, but my husband still knew how to turn on the charm. And he always topped it with a smile, pain and all.

We had our first date night after David's parents took his sister Amber, who was attempting to finish her senior year of college, to the airport. The nursing shift seemed particularly slow, so I suggested we watch a movie.

"I'm game," David nodded.

So for about an hour, David lay in bed and I sat in a chair pulled up alongside him, as close as I could get. I missed snuggling with my husband, being so near to his body that I could inhale his scent. But while I couldn't travel back in time to when we were first dating and giddy in love, cuddling every second we could, I was grateful—oh so grateful— that I could still go on a movie date with my husband. For an hour, it was just the two of us, a rarity, laughing at Joe Pesci's goofy antics and Marisa Tomei's brassy sass in *My Cousin Vinny*. We didn't get to finish the movie because David's parents came back with buttery seafood leftovers. Nourishment trumped entertainment. It didn't matter. To me, we had a moment, the first somewhat romantic one since the accident. And I felt giddy again, like a lover, a wife, a feeling I had been missing.

* * *

Sometime the next day, nurse Verna pulled me aside to chat. She could tell I was distracted. I was. I enjoyed the previous day with my husband, but I was starting to feel conflicted. I barely had any time to myself and felt depleted of energy, even identity. I also missed my kids something fierce. Any spare minute I had absent of company, whether taking a bathroom break or going to and from the hospital to the condo, I'd experience the overwhelming power of guilt from not being with them. It would sneak up, unannounced, then pounce on me with unexpected force. I knew I had to be here in Galveston and take care of my husband, but what kind of mother was I to leave my kids this long? And who knew for how much longer?

While I kept these thoughts private, instead focusing on helping my husband recover, Verna saw right through me. That morning, donning brightly patterned scrubs, she passed by me in the hallway near David's room.

Not even saying hello or asking how I was, she gently grabbed my elbow and turned me in the opposite direction of David's room. "Good morning, Carly," she said sweetly, tucking her short, dark blonde hair behind her ear. "Walk with me for a sec."

I followed her lead into the nurse's lounge. The smell of just brewed coffee knocked out the unit's antiseptic smell. The aromatic java coupled with freshly baked chocolate chip muffins placed in an eye-catching basket on the counter created a homey feel. And aside from the ding of the microwave announcing someone's meal or snack was done, no beeping machines were in sight.

As Verna and I sat down at one of the few small round tables scattered around the room, armed with beverages and baked goods, I let it all out. For the next few minutes, I vented to this wonderful woman all the fears I had, the guilt I felt, the loss of control. And in turn, Verna was quiet, listening intently, nodding every so often.

"You know, Carly," she said after my emotional verbal steam waned. "It might do you some good to get away for a little, a few minutes, an hour. Go to the beach by yourself. Wade in the water. Pray. Cry. Get angry. It's okay, actually really healthy, to release these emotions. You can't bottle up all that you're feeling or you'll end up suffering for it."

I knew Verna was right. I told her I had thought about taking a trip back to Nederland. I had only seen the kids three times this month, and the two and a half hour drive by myself just might do me some good. But the more I thought about it, the more fearful I became. I processed this through with Verna and then burst out crying.

"I'm afraid to leave David. I'm afraid to go home and experience the inevitable rush of emotions from seeing my kids. I'm afraid to run into anyone and feel overwhelmed from more emotions. I'm afraid of walking back through the doors to our home because it's not going to be the same as when I left."

The fears that were squeezing my chest tight turned into a suffocating feeling of losing control. I always felt like I needed to be where I wasn't. If I was with David, I needed to be with the kids. If I was with the kids, I needed to be with David. Whenever the kids would visit, the anticipation of seeing them made me bubble over with excitement, but once they were there and I morphed into Mom mode, swimming in the pool and riding bikes with them, doing my best to be present in the moment. I'd, on occasion, revert to thinking about what I was missing back at the hospital. Maybe something bad, very bad, was happening to David. I told Verna all this, sobbing as my juice and muffin remained untouched.

Verna inched closer to me and put her arm around my shoulders as I simultaneously cried and talked. "I feel like I've lost all the control I once had. I've lost control of my marriage. I've lost control of my children. I've lost control of my job. I've lost control of my life, my household. I feel helpless. I want to fix things but I can't."

Verna nodded and said softly, "Carly, I think you are doing amazing! And you're wise enough to realize that you need to focus on helping David get better and delegating other things to other people who love and want to help you. And frankly, I'm amazed that both you and David have managed to stay so positive!"

Verna tried her best to convince me that I'd done very well during this critical time in life. I appreciated every single word, but I wasn't entirely convinced. My feelings were pretty strong and all over the place. I love what Joyce Meyer wrote in her book *Living Beyond Your Feelings*. She said, "The sooner we learn that feelings are fickle, the better off we are."[10] Having emotions and being aware of them are important. I've said it before and I'll say it again, we're not robots. We are human beings living through real experiences that are hard and sad and traumatic and unfair and all those things. Now, it's one thing to be aware of and to feel whatever it is we feel, but it's another thing to treat those feelings as a god.

I could not allow guilt and fear to overwhelm me. Sure, I needed to be honest with God and with my friends and family, but it was unhealthy for my emotions to rule over me. Beating myself down with guilt didn't do me or anyone else any good.

Before Verna and I headed out of the nurses' lounge, she said something I'll never forget. "You know, Carly, if I were a betting woman, I'd put my money on David. And there's even money in my account! David is an amazing man and I've never, ever, seen anyone with the severity of his injuries do so well and have such a positive outlook. Like you, your husband is incredible."

Her words were deeply encouraging. And to that I smiled, wiping dry my tears.

Walk Through Fire

* * *

Two days before David's sixth surgery, I took off for home for the first time since the accident. David thought it was a terrific idea, as did the doctors and nurses. It was such a reassuring sendoff, you'd think everyone was happy to see me go. As much as it pained me to leave my husband, who was being well taken care of by the nurses and Marilyn, his mother, I was beyond excited to see my kids.

As my car rumbled aboard the ferry, I was anxious to get out on deck. I wanted to breathe in the salty air, feel the warmth on my sallow skin. I left my wife hat at the hospital and before I put the Mom one on, I walked around the large vessel during the fifteen-minute ride, being plain old Carly. I stared out at the tranquil waters watching the seagulls squawk, begging fellow passengers for scraps of the fast food burgers and fries they held in their hands. As waves from passing boats lapped soothingly at the sides of the ferry, I could make out moving objects in the water. I squinted trying to figure out what these bobbing creatures were when I heard some children nearby shriek, "Look, Mommy, look! Dolphins!"

And wouldn't you know it, they were right. A pod of these beautiful mammals, diving in and out of the water with ease and grace put on quite a show for us. I laughed to myself and remembered that on her last trip, Samantha had mentioned that she had seen dolphins on the way to the hospital. I could tell they were a source of comfort the way her eyes lit up when she told me the story. The dancing dolphins were more than adorable sea creatures, they were signs of hope. And not just to Samantha, but that day, also to me.

My trip home was incredible. I was over the moon being able to spend time with my kids as well as my father. No hospital. No restrictions. No visiting hours. Just pure, unadulterated fun. We played board games, one of us who shall remain unnamed trying to cheat their way into a win. We spent hours at the park, competing in swing competitions. We snuggled on the couch and watched movies. I spent every waking minute just loving on my children as only a mama could do. And seeing my Dad in action with the grandkids was a welcome sight. He was doing a great job and I was so grateful for it! Although my Mom had to work back in Minnesota, she did visit with the kids and David whenever she could and they loved whisking away Samantha and Nathan to local fairs and festivals. My parents are amazing people!

Samantha had taken on a lot of responsibility while I was away, often acting as Mommy to little Nathan. She was trying to be strong and continued to put on a brave front. I didn't want her to carry the enormous weight of parenting and did my best to communicate that to her. But as a strong-willed child, I know Samantha was just trying to keep things together in quite a messy situation.

Leaving was hard, complete with never-ending rounds of tears and lingering hugs. But I had to go back. David was scheduled for his sixth surgery and I couldn't miss it. So while Dad resumed the role of main caretaker, I got back on the road and then boarded the ferry, whipped my wife hat out, and as the memories of Candyland and Marco Polo grew dim, I started thinking about David's next round of grafting.

And, once again, a day later and hours after he was wheeled into the operating room, David survived another surgery. His chest and back looked like they were healing well, in addition to the area under his arm that had been covered by skin from his scalp. Only 30-40% of the cultured skin had taken well. The initial report was discouraging news. This cultured skin was so thin that it was hard to even see. It was translucent. In time, more of it regenerated and covered David's body.

Time seemed to be the answer for everything. Day by day, bit by bit, the recovery process bloomed. Though healing wouldn't come overnight, I saw evidence of it throughout each step of the process. I penned this in my journal, always addressing my thoughts directly to my husband:

"My feelings are changing drastically. For the first few weeks, I was always wanting somebody to be able to tell me that you would be okay, that you'd be alive in the morning and that you'd be around for the long road ahead of us. The last few days were a turning point for me. After you came out of surgery so well, I had a sense of peace come over me. I know we're not out of the woods yet, but I have a strong feeling that things will be okay. That you will be here. That we will be able to walk down that long road hand in hand. Such a relief has swept over me!

You're a miracle! We are a part of a miracle! This isn't happening to someone else, but to us....God must have something pretty incredible planned for you and for us!

We are so blessed!"

David

Even with the constant drip of pain medication and vacillating between mental clarity and memory lapses or lethargy, being stuck within four walls all the time started to make me a little stir crazy. My literal view of the world remained unchanged—walls covered with photos or cards, machines, a TV, the door to my room. On special occasions, after helping me out of bed and into the cardiac chair, I'd get wheeled out to the family waiting room, to spend time with whomever was visiting, and then go back to my room.

Chuck and the kids came down the first weekend of October. They hung out in the condo nearby, and I remained in my hospital prison, missing them and wanting to spend time with them.

Later that day I asked Carly if I could go outside. "I see this room all the time," I groaned. "I just want to get out of here and actually see something else!"

She understood and promised to put in a request. "It might be a while," Carly warned.

I nodded. It seemed like "a while" was the standard amount of time anything took to get done, from eating, to sitting up, to taking a few steps. I had to start getting used to this dreaded time frame.

In the beginning of October, David began more intense physical and occupational therapy. It was crucial to maintain range of motion in David's extremities, not only to strengthen his weak muscles but also to stretch his skin. Different types of therapists would come to David's room every day for thirty minutes to an hour. Sheila and Kim, his occupational therapists, helped move around his shoulders, elbows, hands, and fingers. Darren and Sarah were physical therapists who helped bend and extend his legs, knees and ankles. While I wouldn't say he enjoyed these sessions, David was compliant, a very good patient, doing whatever he was told to do. The goal, just like the face exercises, was to stretch his skin. My husband was at their mercy as therapists pulled and stretched his joints. He never complained, not once, though I couldn't help but notice winces of pain in his eyes with every bit of movement.

My dad brought the kids down during this time. I enjoyed their company in the condo while David spent some one-on-one time with his mom and his sister Teresa, who had just flown in from Indiana for another visit. While my Dad and Nathan took a nap, my little girl and I sat on the patio drinking cold root beers and watching the palm trees sway around the glistening community pool. As we sipped our icy drinks, I helped Samantha with her homework, checking her spelling and grammar, listening to her read aloud, and quizzing her for an upcoming test about the Civil War. I felt normal, like a typical mother coaching her daughter through her studies, chatting away an afternoon without a care in the world. That short period of time when our world was just about us was a blessing, a reprieve from surgeries, doctor's report, nurses' orders, and therapy. I loved every moment of it. And I could tell that Samantha did, too.

David's seventh surgery was scheduled for October 4th.

More grafting needed to be done as well as repositioning his hands and fingers to maintain a 90-degree angle. The good news of the ultimately successful surgery was dampened by a bacterial infection. Though it wasn't making David sick, there was a small chance it could infect another patient, so he was moved to a more isolated room in the unit. For me, it was an opportunity to set in action my decorating skills. My husband had made pretty clear that he was tired of the same view day in and day out. The room change necessitated an explosion of a new batch of get-well cards on the wall as well as different photographs from friends and family. The updated décor wasn't what David had in mind, of course. I knew all he wanted was to get out of the unit and take a breather outdoors. How likely that was, I wasn't sure, but I did a fair share of asking, begging, and reminding to make it happen.

One evening, about a week after surgery, I watched Nurse Jim change David's bandages. Jim was a character. A stocky man with a big personality, he loved anything composed by Andrew Lloyd Webber and was just as big of a fan of Enya and played these CDs on the boombox Clyde had given David while working on David in his room. David especially loved listening to Enya, her pure melodic voice and hypnotic melodies fostered a very relaxing environment.

As Jim carefully removed the gauze, I eyed David's skin intently, slowly and methodically rolling my gaze from the bottom of his feet to the top of his Scarlet Red-wrapped scalp. I could tell it looked much better. The last time I saw his skin, it had a dark red appearance, looking more like discolored patches than skin. But this time, it had a pinkish-white color to it, like real flesh. I may not have an MD, but I knew the complexion difference was a good thing.

Almost two months from the date of David's accident, his doctors gave us clearance to take him outside. It was an answer to prayer, especially for my husband. Not seeing actual sunshine in so long would have driven any sane individual bonkers.

Getting him into the cardiac chair was a complex process, thanks to the traction device. Nurses had to lower the contraption and remove the cords, pulleys, and wires that were connected to the pins in his joints prior to situating him in the chair with the help of Nurse Verna, Sarah, Kim, David's mom, and me.

Verna, draped in a surgical gown, placed a sea blue plastic shower cap on David's head to cover his scalp and stayed close to his side while one of the therapists wheeled him out of the BICU, through the hallway, into the elevator and out the doors of the hospital's main entrance. David's mother and I guarded his sides and chatted away with our brave patient, who was covered head to toe in ACE bandages and generously padded by puffy pillows and blankets.

David

The first time I went outside since the accident, I was scared. Doing anything for the first time in a long time can be frightening for good reason. I didn't know what to expect. Would my breathing become erratic? Would my skin react in a bad way? Would the sunlight be blinding? Would I be so overwhelmed that I would beg to turn around and go back inside?

As we got closer to the doors of the hospital entrance, I felt my heart beginning to race. Not in a bad way, though. It was excitement, a good kind of anticipation. The moment the fresh air hit me and swept across my face in a gentle breeze, I felt ecstasy. Alive. Pure. Connected to nature instead of hooked up to machines and shrouded in gauze. I don't remember talking much, but staring at the sky, a soothing shade of light blue, absent of clouds. For the first few minutes I could ignore the hubbub of the parking lot and the visitors streaming in and out of the hospital, the sound and smells of moving cars. Instead I tuned into the flowering hibiscus trees, a screaming pink color that stood out in contrast to the beige hospital and surrounding buildings.

For about thirty minutes, accompanied by my five ladies, we planted ourselves under the awning near the front entrance. Kim used the tranquil setting to get me to do some occupational therapy, moving my arms and fingers around. The time passed quickly, as it usually does when you're in a state of temporary bliss. As I was wheeled back into the hospital I jokingly told my entourage, "Well, now that I know how to get out of here, I'm gonna start working on my escape plan."

Oh, how I wished I actually could.

* * *

"I'm not saying you're going home next week, David, but we've got to start talking soon about getting you to the point where you are well enough to start getting ready to go back home," Verna said, beginning one of her many spirited pep talks. Her bright smile was as wide as Carly's, who stood beside me on the other side of the bed.

I nodded weakly. While Verna didn't offer a specific or even a general sense of a timeline as to when I'd be discharged, she always helped put me in a forward-thinking frame of mind, though never offering false hope. Carly and I had always appreciated her sincerity and her honesty. I took this opportunity to pelt Verna with questions and kept them coming as fast as she could answer them.

"Will I be able to swim again?"

"Yes," she nodded. "Now, it might be a while before you feel like you can do it, but swimming is great for you and will help rebuild your muscle tone and physical endurance."

"What about woodworking?"

"Yup, that should be fine. You'll just need to be careful."

"How about being in the sun?"

"Oh, you'll still be able to go outdoors, but you'll always need to wear sunscreen, every day, every season. You'll also need to wear a hat to protect and shade your head, ears, and nose, as well as long sleeves and pants. You don't want to get too hot since your body is unable to sweat because your sweat glands were burned off. You'll also need to be extra cautious because you don't want to get sunburned.

"What about sensations? What will I feel when I touch things or people touch me?"

"It'll all feel different," Verna admitted. "You'll just have to wait and see how your body compensates. Hot won't feel very hot. Neither will extreme cold. Cuts won't feel like cuts. A pinch may feel like just a gentle touch. So you'll definitely need to be careful."

It felt pretty wild talking about these things. It was only

the end of October. And while I couldn't quite yet imagine my future, it felt like my life was moving. Going somewhere. Inching forward past lying in bed most of the day. And I tried to think ahead, I really did.

But the physically menacing and uncomfortable traction device sometimes made it challenging. Not to mention I had gotten back my glasses during this time. Because I couldn't wear them behind my ears, nurse Rachel had attached them to a pink headband, which wrapped around my head. The feminine color aside, it was a clever idea.

Seeing my mangled hands clearly for the first time in this ungodly contraption freaked me out. I could see where my fingertips had been amputated, the damaged landscape of my hands. And, oh yeah, the traction device. I remember thinking my hands were in hay rakes. Very disturbing.

Something that helped me cope during some tough moments, like whenever I found myself focusing on how badly I was injured or how ghastly my hands looked and, of course, the dreaded tub room, was finding my happy place. It helped me escape reality. I'd travel in a daydream to a wheat field in Kansas, strolling through bales of gold with a Collie beside me, wagging its long tail. I'd walk for miles gazing past the autumn fields at white puffs of clouds stretched lazily across a turquoise sky. I liked my happy place. It was easy to create and stay there.

But then came the dreams. While I was stuck in the traction device, I had a recurring nightmare of being in this fantasy field and walking out to a nearby general store. I'd order a Coke at the counter and whenever the gentleman manning the cash register told me how much it was, I'd fumble awkwardly trying to pull out my wallet from my pants pocket. I never got close because of those darn hay rakes (think Edward Scissorhands). The longer I tried, the louder the cashier became, angrily yelling at me to stop screwing around and pay him. Needless to say, the day the pins came out of my hands was truly a happy place. My father was there when a team of interns showed up manning some large bolt cutters and a drill. One look at these newbie doctors and the handyman tools and panic swept over me. "Are you sure this is standard procedure?" I asked one of them.

"Of course it is," someone replied. Well, at that point I had no choice but to trust their expertise.

I took a deep breath and tried to mentally simulate my golden Midwest wheat field, which worked until one of the interns started the drilling process. Instead of pulling a pin out, he was digging it in further. I seem to recall my father smacking this particular doctor in the back of the head (though I have a feeling that image was the pain meds talking) and barking, "Hey, doc, c'mon now. Lefty loosey, righty tighty!" Dad even grabbed the drill out of the horrified intern's hands and showed him how to switch the button to reverse mode. Not one of the intern's finer moments, I'm sure. But despite the mild drama, I was free of the hay rakes and trapeze-like trappings. Free to endure the healing process without feeling attacked by metal and aluminum.

7.

Hope is the thing with feathers
That perches in the soul
And sings the tune without the words
And never stops at all.[11]

Emily Dickinson

David

"Looking good, David," my father-in-law Chuck said as Nathan wrapped his arms around Grandpa so tight it looked like it might cut off his circulation.

"Thanks, Chuck," I voiced, trying to sound chipper but feeling discouraged. My son wouldn't even look at me. It was the first time I had seen Nathan since the accident. And while I was excited to see my little boy, he was frightened out of his mind.

"It's Daddy, Nate," Carly said soothingly, as I sat in the cardiac chair in the BICU family waiting room, unable to comfort my son other than nod in his direction. The more everyone around him tried to get him to look in my direction, the further he dug his arms into his Grandpa's arms and neck. Talk about heartbreaking.

Then again, it must have been quite a shock for the little guy. One of the nurses had taken the liberty of wheeling me out to the waiting room after the tub room procedure to enjoy some new scenery and help break up my day. Carly and the kids, who had been hanging out there, didn't know we were coming. My wife and daughter were thrilled to see me, Samantha beaming the minute the cardiac chair pulled into the balloon and flower-filled space. Nathan freaked. He didn't recognize me. And he wanted nothing to do with me. It was not a happy reunion.

And then, after only a few minutes, it was back to my drab room.

Carly

Two more surgeries closed out the month of October for David, mainly more grafting, all of which were successful. In Dr. Sanford's words, "David continues to amaze me. He may only have two more surgeries left and that's conservative. His body is about 85-90% covered, or healed." When I asked Dr. Sanford if we were finally past the critical stage in David's progress, he told me we were rounding that corner.

I was overjoyed at how far David had come since the accident. His appetite had increased, he was sleeping better, and doctors had finally removed the feeding tube that had supplemented his required daily caloric intake. We also had another date night, munching on a pepperoni pizza with extra cheese and watching part of *One Crazy Summer*. And best of all, doctors had removed the dreaded traction device.

When the doctors and nurses started talking about David being admitted into a rehab center in the near future, we were ecstatic. As we entered November, the little things that accounted for David's progress were adding up. Nurse Rachel recommended that David's catheter come out. It had been in so long, it had become a breeding ground for infections. For the first time, David even sat up in bed unassisted for two whole minutes. And he was about to start a more intense bout of occupational therapy. Lots of changes. Positive changes. Great things to look forward to.

I went back home to visit the kids for the weekend. We spent all day Saturday at the Fall Festival at church, enjoying dishes from the potluck meal, fellowshipping, and taking photos of the crazy costumes some people wore. On one hand I enjoyed talking to folks I hadn't been in personal touch with for over a month; on the other hand I felt a pressure to explain David's condition to every single person who approached me to wish him and our family well. It's not that I didn't appreciate the prayers or support; it's just that my life was centered on his recovery and being home was an outlet to shift my focus on my children.

When we went back to the house, the kids and I cuddled on the floor, shared a tub of buttered popcorn and watched a movie before I sent them to bed. Tuckered out, they lay sleeping soundly while I plopped down on the couch. I still couldn't bring myself to sleep in the bed David and I shared. As it was, everywhere I looked, I envisioned him being there. I saw him eating breakfast at the kitchen table. I saw him brushing his teeth over the bathroom sink. I saw him moving a heavy box for me in the garage. I saw him getting dressed for work in the bedroom. Memories flooded me and made me miss the life we once shared.

It was tough going back to the hospital Sunday night. The past twenty-four plus hours gave me a semblance of normal. It reminded me how much I missed staying home with my kids. Not that I wanted to rush David's progress, but as I kissed Samantha and Nathan good night and drove back to Galveston, my mind bloomed with hope of David coming home. It would be soon, I believed, praying quietly as I rode down the almost empty stretch of highway flanked on both sides with oil wells and stray cows.

Soon, I whispered in faith. *We're going to get our life back real soon.*

It was a confident prayer, trusting words based in God who is capable of performing the impossible, miracles beyond our wildest imagination. But on some level, it was also a prayer of naivety.

* * *

Sheila, one of David's occupational therapists had stopped by Monday morning, armed with a folder brimming with printouts of exercises, and spent a good hour or two with us going over my husband's new daily OT regimen of many of the stretches and exercises we'd have to continue every day for the next several months. As she modeled with specific instruction how to work out each joint, her adept hands bending David's fingers and arms slightly and in different directions, tension started building in my neck. The scene in front of me started fading as the pain routed into my head. Stress.

Sheila stretched out David's right arm as he grunted.

"One way to know that you've got a good stretch is when you notice the skin over the joint turning white. This is good."

I watched her every move. "Can stretching too much cause any damage?" I asked.

Sheila nodded, David's wrist and elbow now in her capable hands. "Well, there is a balance, of course. You want to stretch the joint to the limit without going too far. If you stretch David out like Gumby, the skin will split and tear. Obviously we don't want to do that."

As Sheila elaborated more detailed instructions on how to push, pull, stretch, and move my husband's body parts, worry set in. I wondered how—even to the point of doubting—I'd be able to do all this once we were home in addition to keeping up with managing the house and taking care of our kids.

Then Sheila gave us a reality check, what we could expect when David would eventually leave the hospital. "Anticipate about six months to a year of rehabilitative therapy, more so towards the latter. But through this process," she said as she began working on stretching one of David's hands, "and with all that work, I'm confident that you'll gain back your gross motor skills like walking and eating with adaptive utensils. And I'm hoping eventually you'll even pull on a pair of pants and a shirt on your own."

As her words sunk in, I felt disappointed. What she was telling us that David would eventually be capable of doing felt so minuscule. I mean, pulling on a pair of pants. Really? And then, in what felt like another killjoy moment, Sheila added, "Frankly, David—and I promise I'm not trying to come across like a doomsayer—but I don't know if you'll ever be able to button a shirt."

My heart fell at first. It was dispiriting to realize that we might not regain all of our life back—that major changes would be necessitated. That I might have to play the roles of nurse and rehabilitation therapist for quite possibly a lifetime. While that reality was initially suffocating, I brought to mind what mattered most. That David was alive.

And as Sheila continued to push, pull, stretch, and move David's limbs, a smile branched out on my face, nudging away the worry. So changes awaited us? Big deal. I had prayed and prayed and prayed for David to survive and he did. And if I had to button up his shirt for him the rest of his life, so be it!

He was, however, able to feed himself, albeit slowly, with a handmade utensil that had a built-in extension allowing him to handle it, even with limited mobility. He was also making grand strides in occupational and physical therapy. Sarah, one of the physical therapists, was helping David sit by himself on the edge of the bed and then stand far enough up to get his buttocks off the bed in a pseudo squat. He would hold position for a few seconds and then sit back down on the bed. After a few days, David was able to stand up straight. Seeing the increase in his physical capabilities after such a short time made me want to do cartwheels down the hallway.

David

I remember when the kids came for a visit the beginning of November. As always, they were a welcome sight. Full of giggles, energy, and love, though Nathan was still a bit distant. I was incredibly grateful for every opportunity to spend time with them. I was able to go outside this time, accompanied by my mom, Carly, my father-in-law, and the kids. It was my second visit to the great outdoors since the accident.

We headed over to the Children's Garden, a tranquil space designed to promote healing for pediatric patients and their families in a natural environment. Samantha gabbed away, sticking close to my side while Nathan trotted on a few steps ahead, holding on to some plastic toy. I found peace in this secluded hideaway, surrounded by tropical flowers and lush foliage. My kids scampered around the garden on an exploratory journey for cool-looking bugs under big gray rocks while I watched them in silence.

As the adults talked to one another and to me, I zoned out of the conversation, focusing instead on Nathan and Samantha who were lost in their imaginative worlds. I wanted to run around the garden with them. I wanted to hug them. I wanted to scoop them up in my arms and toss them high into the air. But I couldn't do any of those things. The limitations I was faced with made me sad and in a big way, powerless. Watching them was a reminder that life had changed and would never be the same. By the time we had to return to the BICU, it was time to eat. But my appetite was gone and my throat hurt. Matter of fact, I hadn't been very hungry the past few days. I couldn't put my finger on it, but something was wrong. I just didn't feel like myself.

Carly

As the first week of November came to an end, David's mother went back home. She had selflessly stayed with us since the accident happened and had been a priceless blessing in this battle. She provided David with a nurturing and motherly comfort that the nurses couldn't provide. She and I were a tag team, giving each other alone time with David while the other took a break. This helped us both avoid burning the candle at both ends. I'll be eternally grateful for her loving presence and support. Kissing her goodbye on the cheek, we made plans to reunite in a couple of weeks at the hospital for Thanksgiving.

Since eventually I would be home with David day in and day out, I had to be fully prepared, equipped, and ready to step up to the challenge of being his main caretaker. And I was. Besides, David was doing so well. Someone even told us that he might be able to move out of the hospital by Christmas and attend a day hospital for rehab, spending nights at a nearby apartment.

It was around this time that David started spiking fevers of 104 and having trouble swallowing. Tests were run and showed that his white cell count was alarmingly low. His red cell count was also down and his electrolyte levels were going haywire. My husband's organs were slowly shutting down. Doctors and nurses, shrouded in plastic gowns, scuttled in and out of the room, running a battery of tests on his eyes, his heart, his lungs, his throat, and his colon looking for places an infection might be hiding. Still, no doctor or nurse had a reason for the sudden downturn. They were all perplexed, lacking answers.

While waiting for test results, all of the tubes that had been taken out of David, like the catheter and the feeding tube, were put back in. I sat by David most of this time, watching my husband deteriorate before my eyes. It was only a few days earlier that we were outside, soaking in sunlight and watching the kids romp around the Children's Garden. It was only a few days earlier that we were talking about rehab centers and getting excited about upcoming talks of a discharge plan and looking forward to possibly coming home by Christmas.

And now here I was, staring at my lethargic husband, covered in the same plexus of tubes and wires that were attached to him when he was first admitted and with the same background noise of hushed tones from the nurses and the barrage of orders for this and that medication from the doctors. The mood had changed, it seemed, overnight. The tension was palpable. The smiles from the nurses who used to joke around with us were replaced with tight-lipped expressions, worried wrinkles. The small talk disappeared.

David's cultures showed he had a life-threatening staph infection, resistant to most antibiotics. But tests didn't suggest where it was coming from or how it started. My husband was getting worse by the hour. When he wasn't lethargic or confused, he was in a trance, eyes open but without expression. And then, the howling started. It was a terrible sound. A laugh, if you can call it that, reminiscent of a nut job character from a horror movie. When I heard it the first time, I froze, my feet glued to the linoleum floor of his room. A nurse nearby had heard the commotion and rushed in to see what was wrong. I stood still, shell-shocked, watching her check the monitors, the IVs, as my seemingly sane husband howled like a hyena.

A tear slipped down my cheek, landing on my shoe. *What was happening to David?*

More tests were ordered—spinal taps, x-rays, echocardiograms, CAT scans. While the doctors suspected a neurological issue, every test came back without a definitive answer, leaving the medical team unable to remedy the infection.

On Sunday, November 14, almost three months since David's accident, Verna pulled me aside. She looked deep in my eyes, the look on her face soft, quiet. She spoke slowly, "You need to call your family, Carly. David's very sick."

I nodded, telling her I would. But everything in me screamed "no." I don't know when or how, but I made the phone calls. And as David's parents and sisters, my mom, Gordon, Jackie, Clyde, and Linda were rushing over to the hospital, I sat with David. Watching him sink deeper, physically and mentally, into what was clearly his mysterious demise.

Keeping vigil at David's beside, without direct communication from doctors, without knowing what was going on, was gut wrenching. It's hard to be hopeful when you're in the dark, chained to the sidelines watching a head-on collision in slow motion. I remember one time praying silently as I watched a once calm David start to squirm in discomfort. Clearly agitated, he started wiggling around so much, the tubes in his body needed to be repositioned. As seconds went by, he got more agitated, trying to pull at whatever object was nearest him.

"C'mon, David. Relax. We're with you. Just breathe,"

Verna whispered, trying to fix the mess he was making, one hand gently stroking his arm, the other finagling tubes and wires. Without even looking over at me, she said calmly, "Carly, I need your help over here."

I stood next to her, waiting for instruction while also trying to soothe my husband. "It's going to be fine, David. I'm here. I love you." My heart thumped uncontrollably in my chest as I did whatever Verna asked me to do.

But David wanted nothing to do with us. Growling like a wild animal, shifting his body violently in bed, he spit in our faces.

Verna remained calm, doing her job as best as she could, but I broke down. It was obvious I was losing my husband. I didn't know who he was. The maniacal laugh, the growling, the spitting—this wasn't David. This wasn't my husband. I didn't know who it was or what was happening, but this wasn't him. Without talking to us or giving us eye contact, David had simply checked out. I didn't feel like he was really there.

I clenched my trembling hands, knees wobbling. *I have to get out of here. I have to get out of here*, my mind raced recklessly. I remember walking the same hallway I used to pace when David was first admitted. The same floor, the same walls that surrounded me when I begged God to save my husband's life, to help him beat the odds. The same refuge where I had retreated to find solitude and cry in private, to let the tears spill down without restraint in the presence of sweet Jesus alone. I was in that same place. Ultimately for the same reason, crying out to God for mercy, for a miracle. I sobbed as my shoulders shook forcefully, continuing to beg the One who I believed had orchestrated David's progress, his recovery. "Save him, Father," I pleaded. "Please save my husband." I didn't understand how God could bring us this far only to take him away from us. It didn't make sense. Nothing about this ordeal made any sense.

I walked back slowly to David's room, experiencing a mental shift with each foot that fell one in front of the other. Maybe I was being selfish. Maybe I was championing for David to hold on, to live, only so I wouldn't have to endure a new life without him. Maybe my husband wasn't meant to be here with us anymore. Maybe it was time for him to move on.

Moments later, as I stood over his bed, watching his chest rise up and down in labored breath, tears fell. David's eyes were closed. Slipping into unconsciousness, where he would remain for days, he seemed peaceful, nothing like the unhinged, growling and howling man I had seen earlier. I whispered softly, close to his face, my skin brushing his, "David, I love you. If you need to let go, just let go. It's okay." I stayed with him, until our family started arriving, their eyes red and raw.

As loved ones gathered in the family waiting room, hugging, crying, and praying, I brought them up to speed. Not providing any answers, as we still didn't have any, but stating all I knew at this point, that he had a life-threatening infection, the cause of which was unknown. It's almost funny. Since David's admission, we were all walking on eggshells, the words from the doctors echoing to "wait and see," that unfortunately, his recovery could take an unwelcome detour. And while my husband certainly had some rough times, that almost expected downturn never came. Ironic that it showed up seemingly the minute we started talking about phasing him out of the hospital recovery stage and into full-time rehab.

The hospital administrator walked into the room at some point. Speaking in the same hushed tone I was getting accustomed to when bad things happened, she suggested all of us resettle in the Mackey Room down the hall.

I looked straight into her eyes, defiant. "No," I said. "We will not."

"Carly, it's best," the woman said quietly. "You'll all have more room and will be more comfortable there."

I shook my head, planting my heels firmly into the floor. I knew all about the Mackey Room, though its door was always closed. It was a private place for family members and loved ones of patients on their deathbed, an invitation-only room. The Mackey Room was almost like a pre-bereavement area, where the pre-grief tears were shed and joined, usually swiftly, with actual mourning. While at first I balked at using the room, eventually all of us did.

Meanwhile, doctors, still flummoxed, were working hard to figure out a cocktail of antibiotics to kill David's infection. Many of the nurses who had worked tirelessly to care for David and weren't on duty at this time were blowing up the phone installed in the Mackey Room. Rachel called from home and spent a few minutes crying with me and wishing us well. Mary told us she was lighting candles at her church for David. Verna had asked her boss if she could come in and work, on her day off.

That night was rough. We all cycled in and out of David's room, waiting for a sign that he was getting better, clinging to one another in prayer, support. While my father was back at our house with the kids and knew what was happening, we hadn't said a word to Samantha other than "Daddy is sick." I didn't want to her to worry and didn't feel it necessary to put her through more trauma by hanging out in the family waiting room veiled by gloom.

None of us slept a wink, stretching out on the comfortable upholstered padded chairs and couches in the Mackey Room, our minds fixed on only one thing—David. He remained unresponsive, seeming unconscious except for the occasional growl or howl. We shared our tears, some of us expressing anger that after all the trauma, surgeries, therapy, and progress, David was now slipping away. A sense of injustice permeated the air. None of us were necessarily throwing up our fists at God, but we were honest. It was unfair. And I, for one, didn't know how to process that. I had many conversations with Gordon during this time and he would always tell me, "This is not over yet. God is sovereign and He does not make mistakes. This is not over."

About a week had passed since the onset of David's illness, when Gordon, who had been sitting beside David in his room, rushed into the family waiting room, his cheeks flushed. "Carly!" he blurted out, barely able to breathe. "He's awake! David's awake!"

I'll be eternally grateful to Dr. Loran, one of the residents, who eventually discovered the source of what was making David so sick and the wonder drug that ended up saving David's life. This doctor had a eureka moment while he researched for hours in the hospital library. While David was battling several different life-threatening infections, Dr. Loran determined he was also suffering from Neuroleptic Malignancy Syndrome (NMS) a rare but life-threatening idiosyncratic reaction to neuroleptic medications that is characterized by fever, muscular rigidity, altered mental status, and autonomic dysfunction. Basically, it was a life-threatening reaction to some of the medications David was taking. David was given a cocktail of different antibiotics and an effective medication to reverse the NMS that was so highly toxic, the liquid actually ate through the IV tube!

Everything changed in that moment, the mood, the heaviness, the sense of doom, all dissipating. I rushed into David's room on the heels of nurses who rushed in before me, calling out for doctors as they sprinted.

Gordon told me that as David started stirring, he opened his eyes, turned to his friend and mentor, and said, "What are you doing here?" And that's when Gordon rushed to get me.

In those first few moments and days of David's lucidity, he was surrounded by doctors and nurses, some who checked vital signs, others who monitored electronic stats. David could talk. He knew who everyone was. He was mentally present, without growling or howling. Within a few days, David was back to normal. His vitals were stable, his numbers looked great, and his range of motion was good. Though he was much weaker, and the option of going to the day hospital was nixed at this point, David was back.

David

My eyes opened to a haze. Fuzzy faces. Distant sounding voices. *Was that Gordon*, I wondered. *Or Nurse Jim?* I tried to focus, but coupled with my blurry vision, I felt groggy, drugged, struggling to maintain consciousness.

"David, you awake? You up?" The burly guy who reminded me of jolly old St. Nick leaned in closer toward my face. *Yup, definitely Gordon.*

I mumbled a weak, "Yeah." And then he scrambled out of the room as if his pants were on fire. *Boy am I tired.*

Carly tore into the room with Gordon and a bevy of nurses and doctors.

"David, David! Oh my goodness! You're awake!" my wife exclaimed, a flood of tears pouring down her face.

All I could do was smile. It was always nice to see her. *Carly, my angel*, I thought. And then, exhausted, I fell asleep, the good kind, not the on-the-verge-of-dying kind.

I drifted in and out of sleep for a day or two, and remembered nothing of what transpired in the past week prior to fully coming to. I was sure of one thing: I had checked out for some time, but never aware that at one point I was dying. And just like that, one minute I was fine, the next fighting for my life. This near death episode set me back quite a bit. The nurses and therapists were no longer talking about discharging me to the day hospital rehab program. I got back on track, physically that is, though I was much weaker.

The day before Thanksgiving, I walked some more, wedged into the elevated walker by Sarah, a physical therapist, who acted as a support. Well, shuffled is a more accurate description. For about twenty feet, from the room to the door, I took slow steps forward, leaning some of my weight on a walker, my father kneeling on the floor, his hand around my ankles to help propel me forward.

I remember Carly, the nurses, even my father beaming with pride, so excited that I had taken these steps. I tried to brave a smile, but couldn't shake the feeling of how depressing it was. I was hoping by this time, I'd be more functional. At least more mobile then walking at what seemed like a half a foot a minute. By the time I collapsed out of exhaustion in bed, with help of course, I looked at my wife and gave her a weak smile. I loved her so much. She was my rock, my cheerleader, constantly encouraging me, dispensing daily doses of optimism. Frankly, I'm not sure if I could have survived this time had it not been for her.

Carly

David and I celebrated Thanksgiving in the hospital with Samantha and Nathan, surrounded by our parents and loved ones. Oh, and enough food to feed the entire Burn Unit for two days. And that's not even an exaggeration. Friends of ours from church and David's coworkers had cooked for us—two smoked turkeys, a ham, buttery mashed potatoes, delicious green bean casseroles, melt-in-your-mouth cornbread dressing, the cheesiest mac-and-cheese, scrumptious strawberry shortcake dripping with glaze, an apple pie you could smell down the hall and more. Pretty much every holiday staple you can think of was on a long rectangular table in the family waiting room. It was quite the celebration, and not just because it was Thanksgiving. We were especially grateful for having come through David's death scare only a week or so earlier. Because we had such an abundant feast, we were able to share it with not just the staff but also some of the patients and their families in the burn unit.

The kids had a blast, Nathan warming up to David a little more. He pranced around his father brandishing a plastic sword, exclaiming. "Me Zorro," Such a boy! Samantha chatted us up with an animated account of her life, taking few breaths as she spoke. I loved hearing her talk. She was so lively, full of spirit. It was a joy just to soak up her presence.

When visiting hours were over and my parents started packing up some food to take back to Nederland with the kids, Nathan walked over to David. With an unusually shy look on his face he said, "Bye, Daddy. I misses you."

Samantha was clearly disappointed in having to leave. I could see the letdown in her big beautiful eyes. Goodbyes were never easy, for anyone. I stayed with David for a while as the family waiting room emptied out, black garbage bags filled to the brim with plastic plates and utensils and scraps of food. Charles Dickens said, "Reflect upon your present blessings, of which every man has plenty; not on your past misfortunes, of which all men have some."[12] David was alive. Alive and well. My kids were alive, safe. The present blessings outweighed the disasters that had happened. And for that, I was very, very grateful.

Before the close of November, David had another surgery. Because extensive grafts were performed on his buttocks area, he had to lie face down for about a week. Nurse Rachel made a special foam wedge for him, affectionately named the "David Bowers Sammich," to provide support while lying on his stomach.

On December 8th, the medical team officially informed us to start thinking about Phase 2, rehabilitation. While day hospital was out of the question at this point, we were given two options. David could either make this happen on the 8th floor of the hospital, at UTMB Galveston's own rehabilitation unit, or we could move over to the Health South Rehabilitation Hospital in Beaumont, about twenty minutes away from home. This new chapter was simultaneously exciting and scary. David and I had become so dependent on the doctors, nurses, therapists and aides it was almost impossible to picture a life without them. But I knew David couldn't stay here forever. Not that he wanted to, anyway. The goal was for David to regain more strength, mobility, and function, to try to become more independent.

The eighth floor rehab unit proved to be a drab place. The lack of windows and sunlight and cramped space reminded me too much of the BICU. The visit to Health South was much more promising. The facility boasted large rooms, windows on almost every wall, brightening up every corner. My head spun, not knowing what to do. Though I liked the cheery atmosphere of Health South, there were pros and cons to each facility. David's mom and I discussed our choices in great length with the nurses and came to a mutual agreement: Health South.

A few days before David was discharged from the BICU, the kids came up for the weekend. Accompanied at times by the children's grandparents, we did some Christmas shopping, pushing our way through crowds while taking in the festive decorations. We also went caroling one evening and saw Santa touch down at a local hotel via helicopter. My father and I took the kids to see *Toy Story 2*, Nathan's first theatre experience, in which he behaved exceptionally well. Then my father took Nathan back to the condo and Samantha spent a few hours with David and me in the hospital, watching *Gremlins* in David's room.

As David lay in bed, sandwiched between my daughter and I who sat in chairs on either side of him, I started to see glimpses of normalcy. What a wonderful feeling. The light at the end of the tunnel that we were cautioned might not exist, the hope that might have proven wasted, the warnings not to peek too far into the future—all these things were obliterated. David was leaving the hospital, not quite going home yet, but on his way to getting stronger, more functional, more mobile, more himself.

God heard our prayers.

8.

The secret of change is to focus all of your energy, not on fighting the old, but on building the new.[13]

Dan Millman

Carly

I stared at my husband's discharge papers, a swipe of ink away from handing them to the hospital administrator and walking away from what had been a life-saving second home for my husband.

Four months ago, I was scribbling my signature on consent forms for emergency procedures, unsure whether or not they would even help David survive. And for the following four long months, my husband was constantly monitored by committed nurses, knowledgeable doctors, and high-tech equipment. All eyes and ears were on David, twenty-four hours a day, seven days a week, tracking his internal and external situations, his vital signs, inputs and outputs—everything.

Feeling overwhelmed, the pen quivering slightly between my fingers, I signed and dated the papers, December 15,

1999. I battled the juxtaposed emotions of being thrilled David was finally well enough to leave the BICU and feeling inadequate about leaving the familiar, the comforts of round-the-clock care. Oh, I had watched the nurses tend to his wounds and change his bandages, and even did a number of facial soaks on my own. But I had never done a complete dressing change. I wasn't armed with enough confidence to make me feel capable. Not that I had to do all that yet, but still.

While the BICU was about survival, the focus of Health South was about getting stronger and more functional. I would no longer be a bystander, watching my husband ride the swells of critical care; I would now need to learn how to be an active participant in his care. And while a part of me was excited, I was also scared to pieces.

Tears fell freely that morning, from me, from David, from the nurses. Verna popped in even though it was her day off. "You better give the next set of nurses a hard time, David, just like you did us," she touted with a smile, wagging a finger in his face.

Rachel hugged us both saying, "There's a light at the end of the tunnel, and it's not a train."

Sheila, too, dropped by for a few minutes. "I'm so proud of you, David," she told him. "Now you better work as hard at Health South as you did with me!"

"Thank you so much for everything," David told each and every person there that day who had taken care of him. "I couldn't have done this without any one of you."

Leaving the BICU that day was, as most goodbyes are, bittersweet. Oh, how I wanted to drag some of the nurses with me as reinforcements, support. But, well, that's just crazy. Franklin D. Roosevelt said, "To reach a port, we must sail - sail, not tie at anchor, sail not drift." My back facing the double doors of the BICU, I walked beside my husband, and my mother in law, gritting my teeth and still swelling with an enormous amount of pride for him. We were sailing, slowly, of course, but still, sailing.

David

I left the BICU without being able to form distinct facial expressions, so I hoped my words and pseudo smile adequately conveyed my gratitude to the nurses and the doctors for their care and support. I was excited to leave, knowing I had beaten the odds and made it this far, alive and on my way to gaining some semblance of functionality. But I was also anxious. I was only a few minutes away from leaving an intensive care unit to go to a rehab hospital where most of the patients were being treated for broken hips and spinal injuries. From what I understood of the facility, Health South's expertise was therapy, focusing on increasing my strength and range of motion. As far as my burn injuries, there wasn't much strategy other than to keep me clean and free of infection. While the facility did have a wound care specialist on staff, who dealt mostly with diabetic sores, no one was familiar with burn care. Kinda scary when you think about it.

Doctors had ordered I leave via an ambulance and gurney, since I couldn't sit up for a long period of time, but I never got the gurney. My head shielded by a dark blue baseball cap, I was rolled out in a wheelchair, albeit in a deep recline position, and pushed up a ramp into an ambulance transport van, more van than ambulance. Carly sat in the front seat next to the driver and my mother followed behind in our car.

The sun had set by the time we pulled into Health South. I was exhausted, and not just the physical kind. Mentally, I was reeling from spending four months isolated in a relatively small space and spending two-plus hours in a medical van, hearing the highway cacophony of blaring horns and speeding vehicles. Not to mention, being uncomfortable from sitting for such a long period of time due to a huge bed sore on my buttocks. We had to stop every thirty minutes so I could be repositioned and make it another half hour without being in total discomfort and pain.

Nestled in a quiet commercial area of town, Health South sat on manicured lawns dotted with an assortment of colorful flowers. The second I rolled into the circular driveway, I caught sight of an enormous Christmas wreath the size of an entire floor to ceiling window and a towering Christmas tree illuminated by twinkling white lights. The holiday decorations were a nice touch, giving the place a homey feel. When the paramedic wheeled me into the entrance, Carly and my mom by my side, I was greeted with thundering applause by twenty or so people, family, co-workers, and loved ones from church who rounded out the lobby, lined with vinyl burgundy-colored chairs and a few side tables. I felt overwhelmed by the presence of so many people supporting and welcoming me into this next phase of recovery.

Despite the boisterous chatter from the group, I heard as clear as day Nathan's voice shrieking, "Daddy! Daddy!" He ran toward me and jumped on Carly. Everyone laughed,

Left: David on top of a mountain in Juarez, Mexico while he was on a youth mission's trip (1993).

Right: The night Carly and David got engaged at the Valleyfair Amusement Park in Shakopee, Minnesota (1993).

Left: Carly and David's wedding day with Samantha (1994).

Right: David and Nathan spending time together (1997).

Above: A family photo shoot while visiting Minnesota. Pictured (from left to right) is Carly, Samantha, David, Nathan, and Carly's parents, Chuck & Rie Dougherty (1998).

Right: Nathan, David, and Samantha at a hotel in Brownsville, Texas (1998).

Left: The Praxair facility where the accident took place in Groves, Texas.

Right: The shower table that was used in the Tub Room at UTMB in Galveston, Texas. Nurses would transport David on this table from his room to the Tub Room.

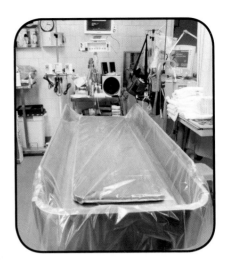

Left: The dreaded traction device —David spent weeks in this position. Here his father, Keith Bowers, leans in to hear what David is saying (1999).

Right: This was the first time Nathan was able to see David after the accident. Taken in the family waiting room at UTMB in Galveston. From left to right: Marilyn, Samantha, Teresa, Keith, David, Carly and Nathan.

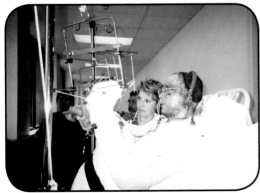

Left: David's first trip out of his room in the burn unit to look out of the windows, accompanied by Nurse Verna (1999).

Left: Carly, David's Mom, Marilyn, Nathan, and Samantha on a visit to the burn unit at UTMB in Galveston, Texas (1999).

Below: One of the first times that David got up to walk after the accident with the help of his physical therapist, Sarah, and his dad, Keith. (1999)

Above: David's physcial therapist, Sarah, helping him stand (1999).

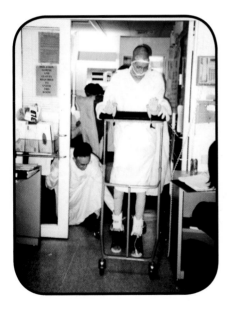

Right: Nurse Rachel with David on the day he left the UTMB burn unit and headed to Health South in Beaumont, Texas (1999).

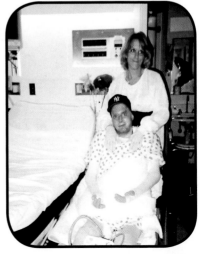

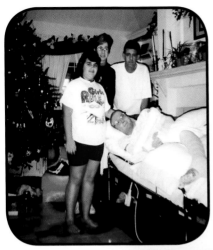

Left: David's first visit home since the accident on Christmas with Samantha, Rie, and Chuck (1999).

Right: David trying to participate in Christmas festivities with Samantha and Nathan (1999).

Left: Because David was unable to sit up yet, Carly rolled the hospital bed to the table and helped him eat the Christmas dinner with the family (1999).

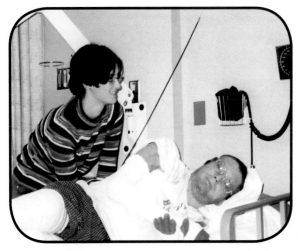

Left: David's sister, Amber, giving him a back rub (2000).

Below: One of the many "Welcome Home" signs along David and Carly's route home from Health South Rehab Hospital (2000).

Above: David and Carly's special date night meal that the cooks and staff surprised them with at Health South (2000).

Right: The Jobst garments and mask that David had to wear 24 hours a day to help with scarring.

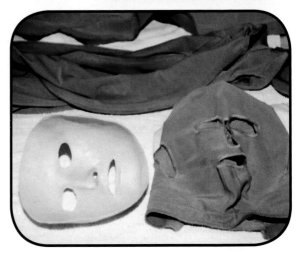

Right: Nathan helping his dad brush his teeth. (2000).

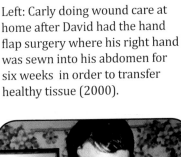

Left: Carly doing wound care at home after David had the hand flap surgery where his right hand was sewn into his abdomen for six weeks in order to transfer healthy tissue (2000).

Right: David standing up with hand sewn into his abdomen (2000).

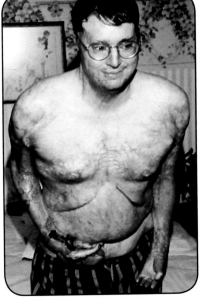

Left: David and Carly hiked Gorilla Rock while in Estes, Park Colorado. This was David's first time hiking since the accident (2005).

Left: A family vacation in Hawaii, with Samantha's husband, Rudy, Nathan, Samantha, David, and Carly (2013).

Right: David and Carly celebrating Samantha's wedding (2013).

Left: Each year, the Bowers family celebrates David's life. They raise and donate money for the Phoenix Society for Burn Survivors. This photo was taken on the 15th anniversary which was an 80s themed party with Rudy, Samantha, David, Carly, and Nathan (2014).

warmed by my son's enthusiasm.

Still reclined in the wheelchair, a foot or two away from the crowd, someone asked me if I was tired. Another asked about the ride. I wanted to keep the mood light, so I answered a few questions with upbeat answers. Then, I noticed one of the higher-ups from Praxair standing in the first row of visitors. Decked out in khakis, a crisp white shirt and a royal blue golf jacket, Tony took a step a forward, smiled at me, and motioned toward Samantha, who was standing near him.

In a loud and booming voice Tony said to the crowd, "I wanted to let you know that Praxair sponsored a contest for children of all employees to submit drawings for a safety calendar."

Turning to Samantha, the man smiled and said, "And I'm proud to say that Samantha was the first runner up! She's got a hundred dollar award coming in the mail and a letter from the vice president of the safety division congratulating her." Extending his hand to shake my daughter's hand, he continued. "And I would personally like to say congratulations to you, Samantha!" More thundering applause exploded in the lobby, this time for my daughter. But the pomp and circumstance wasn't over just yet. Tony pulled out a large framed copy of the award and letter and handed it to my smiling wife for a keepsake.

Her cheeks flushed, Samantha appeared every bit embarrassed and giddy at being fawned over by a room full of smiling, happy people. As artistic as she was, then and now, I had a strange feeling the contest was rigged. But no matter, Samantha reveled in all the fuss, stealing glances at Carly and me as she clutched tight the award, which was outfitted by a shiny blue ribbon.

I hung around the lobby for a few minutes before needing to move forward with the admission process. Pastor Lynne closed out this brief social gathering with a word of prayer. "Lord, we are incredibly grateful for this day and for friends and family who have come. We continue to ask for your healing hand over David throughout this rehabilitative process. Thank you so much that he is close to us. We pray that you'll be with him every single day and that he'll feel your presence with him. We pray in Jesus name."

After the final amen was uttered in a hush, echoing throughout the room, I thanked everyone for coming.

"Okay, okay, David," someone piped up in the crowd. "Good, grief, it's late. Go on and get settled in!" The same paramedic and a friendly nurse wearing bright green scrubs wheeled me through double doors to, as suggested, get me settled.

It had been a long day. But a good one.

* * *

"Two months," said Dr. Smith, a short woman with her long dark hair pulled back in a severe ponytail. She had just finished an extensive assessment of my injuries to formulate a detailed rehabilitative plan. "Realistically, I envision you staying here for two months to gain more mobility, greater function, and increased strength. And through the exercises you'll do here, David, you'll basically learn, or relearn, how to do everyday things."

I nodded, chewing on her words and taking time to process.

"You'll have physical, occupational, and speech therapy every day, sometimes twice. By the time you leave, we'll have you feeding yourself, holding some objects on your own, pulling on some clothes, just to name a few life skills you'll need to re-master."

I continued to nod, thinking how nice it would be to feed myself without using the awkward and uncomely BICU utensil, which though providing me with a creative way to eat on my own, took forever to do. I thought about my hands. Looking down at my disfigured fingers, I wondered how I'd ever be able to flip over an omelet, let alone eat it with a knife and fork.

"And outside of the therapy sessions you'll be doing with our trained medical professionals, you'll also have some homework that you'll need to do," Dr. Smith said with a smile. "Whenever you have a free moment—and I mean whenever—you'll need to work on the exercises you've learned throughout the day. I'm not going to sugarcoat this process, David. It's a lot of work. A lot. But I'm confident that in two months, you'll be well on your way to functioning in real life outside of hospitals." Dr. Smith paused for a breath. "One last thing, understand that you have a long road ahead of you, even after you're discharged from this facility. You'll have years of outpatient therapy and likely several surgeries in the future. So, remember, this is just the beginning."

Boy, that was a lot to take in. But I could only process one step at a time. And my first priority was getting out of Health South as quickly as possible. No offense to the staff or the impressive rehabilitative plan, but I didn't want to stay a day longer than necessary.

"Six weeks," I told Dr. Smith, smiling with confidence.

"I'm going to be out of here in six weeks! You just watch."

I knew it was a stretch. When I was admitted I couldn't do much more than stand with the help of two people, walk about 64 feet assisted by an elevated walker with arm supports, and sit for no longer than forty-five minutes at a time. I also had very little use of my hands. If someone put my adaptive fork in it, I could use it. If someone cut up my food for me, I could then stab it with the fork and bring it to my mouth. I wasn't eating any soup quite yet, though.

My doctor looked amused, but I have a feeling she appreciated my can-do spirit. You need a lot of that when you're trying to rebuild the life you lost.

* * *

After getting settled into the facility, my mom, who had stayed with us since the NMS episode, went back to Indiana. In the first few days at Health South, I was surprised by how unequipped the staff seemed to be to handle my condition as a burn survivor. For instance, I was given a nurse call button, yet I couldn't use it because of my hand limitations so I had to yell for help when I needed it. Also, the first time the nurses did my wound care, their eyes betrayed bundles of nerves. Well, this sure deflated our confidence and provoked more anxiety. Carly and I had to be all ears and eyes making sure nobody did anything to compromise my already vulnerable physical state. Even though the staff at Health South didn't have previous experience with a burn injury, they were very quick to listen to us and they learned how to take care of my wounds.

Outside of eating, hanging out with my family and

sitting with visitors, my days were therapy-loaded. I had a speech therapist whose goal was to get me to stretch my facial muscles and skin so my expressions would be more noticeable. Though considering my other injuries this wasn't a big issue. She'd stretch my cheeks, using her fingers as a human fishhook. She'd also massage my face to loosen up my facial muscles and skin and made me recite the alphabet over and over, sounding out each letter slowly and deliberately. This woman went above and beyond, spending time outside of work hours researching burn injuries and specific facial and vocal rehabilitation exercises that would help.

Vickie, my physical therapist, a petite brunette, worked with me with the ultimate objective of walking without a walker. She was quiet, yet firm. And very encouraging. She sought out ways to lift my spirits and offer hope, and not just by her uplifting words and positive attitude. Halfway through my stay Vicky introduced me to a friend of hers who had been badly burned several years ago. This young man and his wife spent some time talking to Carly and me, offering hope of what was possible. This was her way of encouraging me to continue believing in a good future.

Once or twice a day, Vickie would come into my room and manipulate my limbs to help increase strength and gain better range of motion. My first goal was to move my pillow, which required being able to move my arms in order to reach my head. As she worked on me in the first day or two, she noticed a problem with my knee. It had been quite painful since one of the physical therapists at the previous hospital had stretched that joint a little too far during a therapy session and damaged the ligament; the outer skin across the front of the knee had actually split. I found out later that splitting the skin is a common injury during physical therapy and healing would come with time.

I also had daily occupational therapy, designed to give me better function of day-to-day activities, and included stretching my arms and fingers, neck stretches, splinting my limbs. As I became more mobile, I was able to have therapy sessions in the Daily Living lab, a room full of special adaptive equipment to mimic common everyday functions and tweak fine motor skills. I'd work on my hands by placing wooden pegs into small holes on an upright board.

Aside from therapy, I showered and had wound care every day. Because I had a bed sore, another common hospital issue when you're lying in bed day in and day out, my bed was a commercial grade inflatable mattress. The first time a handful of nurses and aides unbandaged and prepped me for bathing, I lay on the bed as one of the nurses deflated it. The more air released, the more I was swallowed in the now saggy mattress.

"Help me, I'm melting!!" I wailed in my best *Wizard of Oz* wicked witch voice.

Then, I was transported via a mobile shower table to the shower room. With an overhead sprayer and using washcloths or sponges, nurses would with great care gently dab my patchwork skin. As they were unprepared to deal with my type of wounds, I had to teach them the process by walking them through every step. It wasn't a scrubbing or picking off the dead flesh like the nurses in the BICU tub room needed to do. The Health South cleansing ritual and wound care was more of a maintenance thing and, as a result, much less stressful and anxiety-ridden.

I was exhausted after showering, which usually took a grand total of four hours and included redressing my skin. So before another round of some kind of therapy or sitting with a trail of visitors in my room, I'd sleep, and rest up.

Every two weeks, Carly and I would head back to Galveston for a checkup with my burn doctors. The first two times we were transported via ambulance because I still couldn't sit up for a long period of time. Afterwards, Carly would drive us. The BICU visits were pretty straightforward. Whatever physician and nurses were on call that day would take me into the tub room, remove my bandages, examine my skin to make sure it was healing properly, make any dressing or ointment changes necessary, rebandage me, and send me on my way. On occasion, on our way home Carly and I would make a pit stop at a small seafood restaurant down by the seawall and bring fried shrimp Po' Boy sandwiches back with us to eat on the ferry.

On one of my visits I was measured for a beige colored full body Jobst compression garment. After a severe burn, skin can heal in a bumpy and uneven pattern, called hypertrophic scarring. As time passes, this gets worse and causes painful scars and compromised mobility. Wearing compression garments for a long period can help even out the skin. I had taken off my shirt for the fitting and immediately afterward needed to be wheeled to another section of the hospital for a non-related x-ray appointment. Not concerned I was shirtless, I was minding my own business, talking to Carly about something when I heard a woman's voice screech dramatically and very loudly, "Shazam! Were you attacked by a bear?"

When I looked up, my eyes were greeted by a woman,

eyes bulging out of her head like a cartoon character. She scanned my bare upper body up and down, not even attempting to be discreet.

"What happened to you?!!" The question wasn't really a question, but more of an incredulous statement of shocking disbelief.

And that was my first, and not-so-great, experience of encountering a non-medical stranger in the general public. It threw me off guard, made me want to crawl into a ball and bury myself in the ground. I had no response. I didn't even know what to say. Later, thanks to the Phoenix Society for Burn Survivors, I'd be equipped with what to say when people either made ugly remarks or would ask about my story. But that day, I had no tools. And I simply felt ashamed.

Carly

I can't tell you how happy I was to be so close to home, only twenty short minutes away from my children. I could spend nights with them again, feeding them breakfast before I'd head to Health South and spend the days with David, helping with his therapy and becoming more attuned to the extent of care he'd need when he'd be discharged. My dad had planned on continuing to stay with the kids, as long as it took before David came home for good.

The environment at Health South was very kid friendly, at least compared to the strict climate in the BICU, which was understandable considering most of the patients were in critical care. At this new place, not only did we not have to gown and glove up upon entering David's room, the kids could also come and go, even wheeling their Dad around the hallways. Even young Nathan could have more interaction with his dad, other than simply standing by his side and being unable to touch him.

David's room was definitely more spacious than the one in the BICU, more than double its size. His new digs gave ample room to comfortably fit a few chairs and a side table, so visitors didn't have to cycle out of his room so quickly given the lack of space.

Unbeknownst to our kids and the therapists who were working so hard helping my husband gain more function, David and I had set some goals of our own. We wanted to surprise the kids with a home visit on Christmas, once Dr. Smith gave us clearance. I was tired of spending family time in hospital cafeterias, waiting areas, or patient rooms. I wanted us to be together where we belonged—home. I wanted David to inhale the scent of a real pine tree instead of bleach. I wanted him doing something traditional, normal, like watching our kids tear into beautifully wrapped presents. I wanted David to eat home cooked food that came straight out of our kitchen, still hot to the touch. I wanted us to gather in our living room with a newly lit fire crackling in our fireplace.

When that day came, David was on a stretcher and carefully wheeled into our home and on to the hospital bed cushioned with an inflatable air mattress we had ready for his arrival, life took a new course. Only four months ago I was told based on medical facts and statistics that David wouldn't make it. And though I had prayed long and hard—along with hundreds of others—and forged my faith through these pleading words to God, there were times I didn't whole-heartedly believe my husband would ever come home.

But he did. God is so faithful.

David's medical team at Health South helped us transition him home so we could figure out what we couldn't do at home, what we needed to do, and what we needed to change. For the most part, our house was pretty set up for David. But some tweaks needed to be made. We installed a portable ramp from the sidewalk to the front door, put in grab bars by the toilet, replaced the door of the walk-in shower with a curtain, and, of course, we already had the hospital bed in place.

I remember sitting on the living room couch on Christmas day, tossing aside the mess of wires, games, and accessories from the kid's video gaming system that were scattered across the cushy piece of furniture, silently thanking God, over and over and over again for this blessed miracle.

David

"Well, David, here we are," Carly said looking at me with a sheepish grin just as she turned the key into the lock on our front door.

I was laying down on the stretcher not being able to look forward, but seeing the familiar sights to the left and the right. The tall oak tree. Our driveway. A neighbor's car. I took a deep breath when my wife opened the door and I heard the scamper of Nathan's quick footsteps on the hardwood floor and Samantha's unmistakable squeal of delight.

"Daddy!" they both shrieked at the tops of their lungs,

rushing toward the stretcher with superhuman strength. My kids hugged me, their hands gently caressing my bandaged skin. I was all smiles, feeling the overpowering sensation of love.

"Sam! Nate!" I exclaimed, while being wheeled into the living room, inhaling the aroma of ham and cheesy potatoes roasting in the oven and what smelled like freshly-baked, right-out-of-the oven bread, thanks to my mother-in-law Rie, who had come down from Minnesota and did all the cooking. Home. Nothing felt quite as good as being home.

It was great to be back, but it also felt weird, the emotion stemming mostly from the fact that I couldn't do much more than lie down in bed. I watched Carly, Samantha, and my in-laws dart from kitchen to living room, setting the table, carrying dish after dish of our delectable feast, making sure we had enough napkins and serving utensils. I watched Chuck carve the juicy ham. I watched my wife pile on cheesy potatoes, the steam rising from the melted butter, onto my plate. I watched Samantha struggle to twist open the cap on her juice and ask her mom for help.

Note the operative word here: watch.

The issue that loomed when I left the BICU was defining the new normal I could expect in light of my injuries. And while Verna and other nurses had been encouraging and with confidence relayed that eventually I would learn new ways of performing basic skills, that Christmas I could do nothing. Nothing except watch. Nod. Stare. And talk, of course, though I was quiet most of the time. Like a creepy eyewitness.

"Daddy, look at what I got," Nathan would gush after opening each gift, holding up a new toy or video game for me to see. And then, in that same breath, he would turn to Chuck and say, "Grandpa, can you help me open this?" I smiled and nodded, trying to hide my disappointment.

"Look at this," Nathan continued to exclaim as the festivities continued. He whipped out two *Star Wars* light sabers, brandishing them in my face and then handing one over to his grandfather to play.

As the two of them engaged in a low contact battle, I sipped on a can of Boost that Carly aimed at my mouth while showing me one of my gifts. I tried hard to fight back the tears but I was struggling with the loss of my independence. Still, the smile remained pasted on, plastic. There was no way I was going to ruin Christmas because I was overwhelmed at not being able to participate.

Being home for the holidays proved to be both enjoyable and disheartening. Toward the end of my almost five-hour stay, watching my kids ride around the living room and hallway on their shiny new bikes, I was determined to get better quick. I needed to start moving and walking and opening and holding things.

Time is no respecter of person or circumstance. Life was passing by, and quickly. No matter how extensive my injuries, no matter the hard-pressed reality of my limitations, I was not going to be a spectator in the lives of the ones I loved most. I was not going to give up. Armed with this newfound strength of will, I fixed my mind to attack every therapy session with a vengeance, despite how tired or weak I felt.

* * *

By the end of the first week in January, I started noticing

the strides I was making in therapy, the fruits of my labor. By this point, most of my rehabilitation sessions were conducted in the therapy gym, a huge room filled with two neat rows of six wide, flat tables, as well as high tech equipment, weight machines, and large bouncy balls. Patients of all ages and with all types of injuries occupied this gym alongside me, learning how to function, move, walk, lift our arms, and use our fingers. Being in such a public environment with more patients around me made me feel a little closer to the outside world. As was the fact that I could finally wear regular, or what nurses playfully called "big boy" clothes (elastic waist sweatpants and T-shirts) over my dressings. Frankly, I don't think anyone would appreciate seeing me move my legs while donning a flimsy hospital gown three sizes too big.

Spending hours a day in the gym, I grew stronger. Not only could I finally move a pillow, my flexibility had also doubled. I could touch my nose, put on my glasses, and even feed myself without the help of that wretched looking utensil device. I was even able to eat popcorn again, a Bowers nightly snack staple. It was messy but I could do it. As far as mobility, I could walk as far as 322 feet with the walker and even roll from side to side in my bed on my own. Best of all, I was finally able to hold Nathan while he sat on my lap.

And I did my homework, using a few minutes every day after 8 p.m., the end of visiting hours, to complete all homework assignments. I moved my toes. I flexed my legs. I wrote out the ABC's with my ankles. I moved my arms. There were some days I was too wiped out to do every exercise recommended, but I tried my best. Frankly, I had more homework than there were hours in the day.

I saw the kids a lot more than I did in the BICU. Samantha and Nathan came regularly, sometimes sharing their fast food lunches with me, sometimes watching movies. I remember one time Carly was holding Nathan while I lay in bed doing my arm exercises, rotating my one arm around and up and down. My skin itched a ton during this time and Nathan, noticing my feeble attempts at trying to scratch, started rubbing my Ace bandaged-wrapped arm along with Carly's help.

"Feeling good Nate," I told him. "Keep up the good work."

Nathan was quiet, still rubbing my arm and looking deep in thought at me.

"That's some good stuff," I said, encouraging him on a job well done.

He kept looking at me and then stopped rubbing and put his arms around Carly, nestling his head in her neck and pointing to the pictures tacked on my wall. "Look, that's me," he told us proudly. Two-year-olds don't have the greatest attention spans.

Carly, wanting to nurture more interaction between Nathan and me, had taken off the blankets that were covering me, making a big deal that I was wearing pajama bottoms. My boy squirmed out of his mom's arms in delight and jumped down to the foot of my bed, tickling my bare toes and tugging at my pants.

"Hey," I cried out. "What are you doing with my toes, Nate?"

Nathan just stood there with a huge grin on his face and proceeded to tickle my feet even more, giggling as I made an Oscar-worthy theatrical display of how ticklish it was.

Then, I had an idea.

"Hey buddy. Can you go find my beach ball?"

"Yeah, Nate," Carly chimed in. "Dad wants to play catch."

My son's eyes lit up as he ran to the closet, grabbed the brightly colored inflatable ball, and ran back to the edge of my bed, throwing the ball at me with delight on his final stride. We didn't spend more than a minute bouncing the ball back and forth, a form of exercise, as Nathan shifted gears and focused his attention on kicking the thing around the room.

An abandoned and gleaming toy car in the corner of the room captured his attention, my little boy dropped the ball, it bouncing to a pathetic stop at the far end of the room. Playtime was over. Samantha was quick to take Nathan's place. "I'll play with you Dad!" she chimed. My daughter was patient, a smile pasted on her face the entire time, as she threw the beach ball to me. It took quite a bit of time for me to finagle a grip on the thing with my forearms. It gave Samantha and me an opportunity to bond and helped with my function and coordination. Everyone wins!

Mobility was just one of my goals at Health South. Since the accident, I was 70 pounds thinner and had to pack on some pounds. At only 145 lbs. on my 6'1" frame, I looked like a rail, gaunt and thin. Lucky for me, the food at Health South was much better than the hospital in Galveston.

One night, a few minutes before dinner was to arrive, Nurse Carolyn dropped by.

"Hi David," she said with a cheery smile. "When is Carly coming back?"

"She's on her way," I replied. My wife usually ate dinner with me, helping cut my food for me and making sure I gobbled up every bite.

"Great! Well, we have a bit of a surprise for you guys," Carolyn said in her signature raspy voice with a wink.

My curiosity was definitely piqued. "Oh really? And what is that?"

"Can't say, David. It's a surprise! Just let me know when Carly gets in." And with that, Carolyn turned her heels and headed back down the hallway.

That night, Carly and I enjoyed an incredible meal of shrimp, steak, and potatoes, the surprise orchestrated by the hospital chef and the nurses. I can't describe how grateful we were. I imagine the Health South kitchen didn't stock any shrimp in their fridge, so I know someone made the effort to go out and get it. We were thrilled and savored every bite. The only downside to the meal was the can of Boost that sat on the tray next to a bottle of A-1 and a pink vase holding a delicate red rose. That sucker still managed to show up on every food tray that was served, date night and otherwise.

Carly

The second week in January, David and I went back to the hospital in Galveston for a checkup in the BICU tub room. David's skin had started to itch terribly, a common side effect of burns and grafts. Different parts of his body would itch at different times and whoever was visiting with him or closest to him at the time, would volunteer to rub or pat the areas to find some relief; scratching was out of the question because of potential skin tearing. After getting basic wound care, we spoke with Dr. Sanford and asked what we could do about that one particular problem.

Dr. Sanford looked at us with a twinkle in his eye. "Okay, I know this is going to sound strange and you might even think I'm crazy to suggest it, but Preparation H will help."

"What?" David cried. "But I'll shrivel up like a hemorrhoid!"

During this visit, David also got the two full body Jobst compression garments and a silicone face mask he was measured for earlier. A nurse or rep from the company helped him maneuver the suit over his body. When he saw the skintight garment on for the first time, his eyes immediately clouded with disappointment. "I look like a freak," he whispered, covered head to toe in an outfit that made him more of a target for curious stares, especially with the silicone mask that covered his entire face except for his eyes and mouth.

"It's fine, David. I mean, the mask isn't great, but it's part of the recovery package," I said feebly, trying to encourage him.

David nodded, weakly. When we returned to Health South that night, we were both in tears. My husband's defeated spirit was palpable when Nurse Carolyn walked into the room. Trying to lighten the mood she said, "Well, David, I guess you won't be walking into any 7-11s or banks any time soon." We both chuckled, though still feeling crummy.

The garment and mask were so tight and odd-looking, David actually had to carry around a physician-administered medical ID card that stated this garment was purposed for a medical condition. He would end up hating to wear the mask so much he only wore it at night or at home. It made him feel way more insecure than actually exposing his face in public. He wore the full body garment for about a year and a half. While it was a nuisance, it did help protect his skin from getting banged up and helped with the scarring.

Since the accident, David had asked a few times what he looked liked. And the answer each time was more or less the same, "Great!" or "Handsome as ever!" But one afternoon sometime in the middle of January, as we were ready to dive into a meal in his room, David asked me, "Carly, I'd like a mirror."

I paused and then nodded. "Sure, David. Let me see if I can ask one of the nurses to find one for you."

As I walked toward the nurse's station, I remembered the big debate back in the BICU of whether or not to give David back his glasses when he was able to wear them on his face. I wasn't sure. It's not that I didn't want my husband to see clearly. I just didn't know if he was quite ready to see a version of himself that was nothing like the former. Would it make him depressed? Discouraged? Would it set him back psychologically? After much discussion, Rachel had put her hand gently on my arm and said, "Carly, it's time. Sooner or later, David is going to need to see and start dealing with his injuries and his appearance."

Back at Health South, my fingers wrapped around the long handle of a plastic oval mirror, I walked back towards David's room. The closer I got to his bed, the more my hands shook. I was nervous.

"Well, I found one," I said to my husband, trying to sound chipper as I held the mirror up to his face. Silence engulfed the room for a minute, a long minute as I waited for his reaction.

David finally started nodding and a smile slowly stretched out over his face. "Not bad," he responded, moving his head left, right, up, and down to get a good look from every angle. "Not bad at all! I mean, I've never been good-looking to begin with, so I think I look great! Even missing an ear and all!"

I couldn't help but grin. Of course, I always thought of David as good looking, before the accident and after. "I love you," I told him, stroking his head and planting a kiss on his check. "I always have and I always will."

David

I remember staring at my own reflection, looking at my skin. It was red, bumpy, some parts scaly and scarred. My scalp showed a good amount of peach fuzz where my hair was starting to grow in and my face revealed scabs that were healing. It took a minute or two to absorb my new look. While I didn't look like the David I once knew, I also didn't look like Frankenstein. All in all, I was pleasantly surprised. After Carly left, I spent more time studying my face to come to terms with what I saw.

I came home a total of four times during my stay at Health South. But unlike the brief visit during Christmas, I was given day passes the last three times and instead of arriving via ambulance I was able to ride in our truck, a blue Chevy Silverado. Getting in and out of the truck with Carly's assistance (my woman was getting some biceps on her), took about fifteen minutes and was pretty painful.

Days before the second visit, I spent much of my therapy sessions taking the pilgrimage from my room to my truck in the parking lot. I shuffled step by step using the armrests on the elevated walker cheered on by Carly and Vickie, and made my way down the long hallway outside my room, into the lobby, and out the front entrance to the parking lot. Carly always stood behind, her hands holding the ends of a bed sheet tied around me. In case I stumbled, she could catch my fall with the sheet rather than grab my fragile skin and cause unnecessary damage.

My home visits would last several hours. I'd start my day at Health South, get showered and have wound care, spend the day at the house, and arrive back at the rehab facility in the evening. At home, I'd either hang out in bed or eventually in a recliner, outfitted with a wooden platform base made by my father, which made it easier for me to get in and out of. I'd get around the house with the help of a wheelchair or walker. Going to the bathroom was quite a feat and required Carly's help (not fun for either one of us).

On the second home visit, I felt more like Dad, playing with the kids, laughing and messing with them instead of being quiet and helplessly laying around. I remember asking one of the therapists early during my Health South stay how I could get down on the floor and play with the kids on their level. Whoever it was at the time shook her head and voiced a firm, "No. Absolutely not!"

I then asked, "Well, what am I supposed to do if I fall down?"

"Call 9-1-1," was her response.

I didn't let this conversation discourage me and started plotting ways to play with my kids on my own. And I did.

For instance, if Nathan was working on Legos on the dining room table, I could scooch my wheelchair up to the table and play with him. And angled from bed, I could play video games with both my kids.

I remember with fondness the first time Samantha and I engaged in a Tetris war. My daughter sat cross-legged on the bare floor, her fingers curled tight around the Nintendo 64 controller, manipulating the joystick with fury.

"I got a row, Dad," she yelled. "I got another row!"''

Clad in pajama bottoms and a grey T-shirt, I cheered her on from my bed right behind her, holding on to the second player controller, purposely curtailing my Tetris expertise so Samantha could come out the victor.

"Look, Dad, check out what I'm going to do with that purple block," Sam exclaimed, manipulating the joystick to maneuver the bright purple L-shaped blocks and neon green squares that swiftly shot down the screen.

Normally a pretty competitive guy, I had no desire to win or even the score. I was relishing simply having fun with my little girl, finally able to do something with her other than watch. It was a good feeling.

At night, I'd wheel my way over to Nathan's room and read to him from the *Icky Bug Book*, managing to hold the book and even clumsily turn the pages, sometimes with Nathan's help.

Home visits were so much fun. While I wasn't playing hide and seek or riding bikes with my kids around our neighborhood, I was becoming more active. I wanted to rebuild the bond that, given my absence, had waned since the accident. And in small ways, the signs of that happening were evident. Being apart from the kids for so long and being limited physically forced me to learn new ways of interacting with them. There was a learning curve, believe me. But I was figuring it out, one visit at a time.

But there was something else I desired besides reestablishing a relationship with my kids. I wanted my wife back. I know, it's a strange thing to say, isn't it? After all, Carly had been my support, my cheerleader, my anchor during the last tumultuous five months. She was always there, ever present, hardly leaving my side. And it wasn't that I wasn't grateful. I was. I'd be a fool or an idiot not to appreciate everything about her. But the more clarity I gained of the picture of our new normal, the more I realized Carly was stuck in the role of a caretaker. And I didn't need another nurse or physical therapist. I needed my wife.

Carly would stand near my bed, lean in close and help with my rehabilitative exercises. "Bend your fingers," she'd say, helping manipulate those small digits. She'd faithfully encourage even the slightest movement. "Way to go, David. That's it!"

I didn't say it at first, but I'd think, "No Carly, I don't want you to move my fingers. I want you to hold my hand."

I was tired of being a patient. It was time to be a husband, to find a distinction in who we were as a husband, a wife, lovers. One weekend, still at Health South, Carly and I had a date night. We watched *The American President*. As the credits rolled, we found ourselves in tears. It was one of the first nights in a while we were alone, no kids, no nurses or doctors popping their heads in. It was crystal clear that night, for the both of us, that Carly and I were so focused on rehabilitative therapy, we had forgotten about us being husband and wife. The romantics of our relationship had dissipated. Not only wasn't there much "we" time, but skin-to-skin contact was almost impossible, making any kind of intimacy almost impossible. Covered in the tight Jobst garment, Carly could only touch my face. And it's not like I could reach out and touch my wife. Oh, we'd smooch from time to time, but it wasn't anything that would ignite a sexual spark.

It was difficult not to be able to touch my wife, to hold her hand, to caress her cheek, to feel her skin. I missed being intimate.

"I feel guarded," Carly opened up, after we sat in silence for a bit. "I think I've put up a wall. David, for the longest time, I didn't know if I'd ever get you back and so early on, I closed myself off intimately, and probably even emotionally," she admitted, tears in her eyes.

I nodded, listening intently.

"That's why back at Galveston, I was so overwhelmed when Rachel said I could kiss your face. Emotionally, it almost felt like making love for the first time."

"I just miss you, Carly," I said. "And I want you to know that."

"I miss you, too, David," my wife's voice shook a bit. "It's hard...this is just so hard for me. I mean, the day of the accident, we had our perfect little life and it was so suddenly yanked out from underneath me. I don't know how to go back. I just don't."

It was cathartic for both of us to voice what we were feeling, though the conversation trailed off unresolved. Some things can't be solved in a few sentences or even overnight. There were so many aspects to the recovery process that we were beginning to realize at Health South. And unfortunately, at the time, we didn't have a road map on how to navigate through this unknown terrain. As time passed, Carly and I would work together, winging it. I remembered what the doctor had said when I was first admitted to the rehab hospital. "You'll have years of out-patient therapy and likely several surgeries in the future. So, remember, this is just the beginning."

This was just the beginning, and not just for my skin and muscles and limbs. It was also a new beginning for my relationship with Carly.

9.

> *"He gives power to those who are tired and worn out; He offers strength to the weak. Even youths will become exhausted, and young men will give up. But those that wait on the Lord will find new strength. They will fly high on wings like eagles. They will run and not grow weary. They will walk and not faint."*
>
> **Isaiah 40:29-31 NLT**

Carly

I drove down Highway 69 with the window down, a soft breeze blowing through the car. A full moon lit up the sky, casting a soft glow through the windshield. I sighed and turned down the volume on whatever the radio was playing at that moment. My heart was heavy, unconcerned with melodic harmonies, poetic lyrics, or foot-thumping hooks.

Knots formed in my stomach and a lump in my throat. Only a few hours earlier one of the doctors at Health South mentioned the possibility of David coming home soon, as in a week or so. This meant he'd continue with rehab in a day hospital, from 9 a.m. to 4 p.m., and stay with us the rest of the time with the help of home health aides on the weekends. It was great news, right? I mean, of course it was. This is what we'd been waiting for.

I breezed past large green exit signs directing fellow highway companions on their way, my mind simmering with thoughts of the dreaded unknown, which seemed to be the running theme of the journey.

Safety. Security. Protection. These were all elements to my relationship with David that I had once treasured, throughout our five-year marriage. Being a single mother, these were important characteristics in a spouse, far above the other fluff, like being romantic, having culinary skills, or sporting bulging biceps. David had always made me feel safe, secure, protected.

I was used to having David around to take care of our family, to forcefully wield a baseball bat if bad guys invaded our house at night, to fix clogged toilets and maintain lawns, to install and repair large appliances. And while we were grateful for the miraculous fact that David was still alive, he wasn't the same. He was limited. He couldn't provide the extent of safety, security, and protection we were so used to. And what he could end up doing as time passed and with more rehabilitation, who knew?

Samantha was starting to feel the effects of this change. When David was admitted to Health South and I started spending more time at home, I noticed that our daughter was obsessed with feeling safe. She'd frantically check the locks on the door. She refused to let David out of her sight. She'd pester me with the same questions of how we were going to pay our bills and who was going to do our taxes. Our little girl had done a great job of harboring a brave and strong front, but every now and then I could see glimpses of fear peeking through that survival mechanism.

I thought of little Nathan. While he was too young to

remember his dad before the accident, I worried about what their relationship would look like going forward. Sure, our son was warming up to his dad, but would David be able to play trucks on the floor with his boy one day? Or tinker in the garage with him on woodworking or other projects? Or take him on piggyback rides around the house?

Gosh, I hate driving, I muttered as I pulled into the driveway. The time of still and silence had an annoying habit to push my brain into overload. All the things I didn't want to think about would spill over and flood my consciousness. My mind overflowed, nearing the brink of feeling out of control.

Pull yourself together Carly, I whispered.

I sat in the car for a few minutes, my head resting on the steering wheel, feeling the touch of cool leather on my forehead. I muttered a prayer. The help-me-kind.

"Lord, help me to focus on what I need to focus on. Give me strength. Help me not to worry about tomorrow, about the future. David is in your hands. I am in your hands. Our children are in your hands. And that's what matters." As I talked more to my heavenly Father, surrendering the unknown and laying down the questions, I took a deep breath. As my lungs deflated, I felt the weight of an undefined future slip away, quietly, into the humid air of the drowsy neighborhood.

I finally walked into the house, closing the door behind me without the slightest bit of noise so Samantha and Nathan wouldn't wake. I smiled as I tiptoed past my dad sprawled out on the couch, an open newspaper cradling his belly and his fingers still curled around his glasses.

Tomorrow was another day, a new one. I didn't know

the script that lay ahead. I didn't have a blueprint or even a detailed plan. But my hand rested in God's. Armed with knowledge that He had brought us this far, I knew in my heart He'd continue the journey with us. Leading us one day, one footprint, one prayer at a time. I love what Joni Erickson Tada wrote, "Faith isn't the ability to believe long and far into the misty future. It's simply taking God at His Word and taking the next step."[14]

It was time for that step, for David to finally come home.

David

"I told you I'd only be here six weeks," I said, grinning proudly at Dr. Smith who had admitted me to Health South in mid-December. It was January 31, 2000 and I was being discharged.

She smiled. "I'm proud of you David. You've done well here and it's time to move on to the next step. The plan for the next month or so is to attend day hospital and then it's on to outpatient rehab. Day hospital means Monday through Friday you'll continue to receive therapy and wound care at our inpatient facility from 9am to 4pm. And you'll get to spend most of your afternoons, nights, and weekends at home."

Our conversation was brief but hopeful. Physically, I was doing well. The latest checkup I had at Galveston proved a success. My skin was continuing to properly heal, and I had gained twelve pounds in two weeks, confident the required daily intake of Boost would be history (miracles do happen). I'd still need a lot of tending to, thus the necessity of going to day hospital, but I could sleep in the comfort of my own home. I could wake up to the smell of sizzling bacon in my own kitchen. I could tell Nathan bedtime stories every night. I could help Samantha with her homework before dinner. I could even go out with my family to a restaurant and order from a menu.

Before I was discharged, three home health aides were trained on how to do bath care and wound care. Tending to me over the weekend and alternating shifts, whoever was on duty would be responsible for removing the Jobst suit and the dressings covering my entire body, helping me into the shower, gently washing and scrubbing my body with water and a mild soap, drying me off, removing the dead/flaking skin, applying the medicated ointment, rebandaging my body, putting on a clean Jobst garment, and dressing me. Needless to say, it was a lot of work.

At 4:15 p.m., after physical therapy, a shower, and a dressing change, Carly and I left Health South, our pickup truck brimming with colorful balloons, boxes of cards, movies, a boom box. I was excited to come home, but some of the thrill was tempered by reality. Like the fact that walking was tiring. True, I had gotten stronger and developed considerable stamina since starting my rehab at Health South, but using my weakened muscles and trying to keep my balance a few hundred feet was still exhausting. By the time Carly helped me up into the truck, I plopped my head back on the seat rest, my breath heavy. I closed my eyes right at the start of the twenty-minute ride, enjoying the brief respite before I'd have to do it all over again.

About ten minutes into the trip, Carly blurted out excitedly, "David! Oh my word! Look!"

I opened my eyes and was greeted by a large, poster board-sized sign decorated with crosses and yellow ribbons that said "10 Miles To Go" in big, black letters. I smiled to myself as Carly giggled. Something was up, something good that was starting to take the edge off my fatigue.

"And look, another one," my wife exclaimed. Five miles away from home, another colorful sign was tacked onto a telephone pole, this one larger than the first. "Almost Home!" it read, long pastel ribbons glued on and swaying in the breeze. More signs were posted at mile three and mile two and finally, a huge white sign the size of a living room rug bordered by thirty or so pink, blue, and yellow balloons blared "St. Charles Welcomes You Home, David. 1 mile to go." St. Charles was a local Catholic church attended by one of our friends, Jack Fitch. The kids from this youth group had helped us with yard work while I was in the hospital. Amazing how a community of different people, different faiths, can unite to help those who need it. Truly, any religious denomination that acts in this way exemplifies the Church that Jesus came to build.

I could see Carly's eyes welling with tears. As (ahem) masculine as I am, I felt my eyelids brimming with some of my own. As we rounded the corner of our street, two girls from our church's youth group, smiles sweeping over their faces, jumped up and down on the sidewalk at our arrival. Carly and I waved, slowly rolling down the street and into our driveway as they chased us on foot.

Still sitting in the truck as Carly leapt out of her seat to fetch my walker, I scanned home base. Dozens of folks from our neighborhood, from our church, and from work gathered in the front yard, waving and smiling. On our lawn, which was mowed and trimmed by the kids, perched twenty plastic pink flamingos (an inside joke shared between Carly and me and the youth group kids).

Bundles of yellow balloons were tied to the top of the mailbox and flanked the sides of the garage, on which hung a colossal aqua-colored banner that read, "Welcome, Dave!" Another sign next to it said, "It's a bird. It's a plane. It's Super Dave!"

Everywhere I looked, my eyes would catch sight of a flamingo, balloon or a sign telling me:

"We're glad you're home!"

"We love you, Dave!"

"Dave, you're our hero!"

By the time I swung my legs over the side of the passenger seat and Carly helped me out of the truck and into a standing position in front of the walker, everyone who showed up for the homecoming gathered in a tight group in front of us. They started clapping, hooting, and hollering. The clamor echoed throughout our mostly quiet suburban neighborhood, sounds reminiscent of a good party.

"It's good to be home," I said with a smile, feeling kind of silly that I was wearing a bed sheet tied around my waist.

"Wow!" is all Carly could mutter as she wrapped her arm around mine, and our friends and loved ones started snapping pictures.

I felt overwhelmed. Loved. Supported. Cheered on. I'd heard about all the prayer requests and well wishes. Day in and day out, I'd stare at the flood of cards and letters and emails tacked up in my hospital rooms. And though only in bits and pieces while in the BICU, I remembered some folks who stopped by to visit. But now, standing in the driveway of my own home, I was finally seeing a crowd of real faces, smiling, happy faces who were rooting and praying for my recovery. This reminded me that we weren't alone. The scene was so emotionally overpowering, I was almost rendered speechless. But I knew I had to say something.

"Thanks for all the support, everyone. Carly and I appreciate it," I said after the applause died down, my voice cracking from emotion. My wife kept her head down. I know she felt just as overwhelmed as I was. Her tears splashed down on the asphalt, landing near her tennis shoes.

There was silence for a minute. I didn't know what else to say. Frankly, I was afraid the waterworks would gush and I'd ruin my masculine image. Not a picture I wanted to leave with these wonderful people. Thank goodness Pastor Lynne saved the day.

"Guys, let's all join in prayer," she interrupted, walking to face the crowd. "And then we can leave and let Carly and David go inside in peace." Pastor Lynne offered a beautiful prayer and after uttering "amen", she shooed us toward the house with her hand and said, "Now go." We all laughed and while Carly and I started up the walkway to the front door, our friends headed on their way, blowing kisses and waving goodbye.

What a homecoming.

Carly

As David and I closed the door behind us, we both exhaled. I felt bad because I didn't say more than a sentence or two to some of the folks who peppered our yard. There was a lot

I wanted to express, but I just couldn't do it. I felt trapped in this weird feeling, much like being stuck in the *Twilight Zone*. It seemed our world, the Bowers' microcosm, had stopped for six months, while the world around us and everyone else in it continued to spin on the axis of life.

We'd been home before and made baby steps to transitioning into semi-independence. So while I didn't feel like we were pushed out of Health South with the frightening understanding of swimming or sinking, David and I were beginning to re-engage our roles as Husband, Wife, Mom, and Dad, together, in partnership, though my dad was still at the house with us, helping with the kids.

Stepping foot in our home that day, seemingly again for the first time, I was on a mission. I wanted to prove that we could handle this new life. That we didn't need to rely on a village anymore. I didn't know what to expect—what's new, right?—but I was ready for the challenge.

* * *

Two weeks into our new normal our days had been pretty consistent. Packed, but regimented. Samantha went to school. Nathan was in daycare part-time. And David and I spent the day in Health South's outpatient rehab program. Aides popped in on the weekends to take care of bathing and wound care. This was a transition period for David and me, giving us baby steps to eventually having him home with us most of the day.

I pitched in at times, helping clean up David whenever an aide wasn't around or called in sick or something. It wasn't fun. Don't get me wrong. I'd do anything for my husband, anything. But touching him, especially changing his bandages hurt him. And that, in turn, hurt me. I'd peel back the gauze and cry. A good portion of the material stuck to his skin and needed to be pulled off, but with just the right amount of force that his skin didn't come off in the process. This was a tough balance.

"I'm sorry, David," I told my husband the first time I changed his dressings, tears falling down my cheeks. "I know I'm hurting you." Used bandages piled up on the table beside me, pieces of scaly, dead skin accumulating quickly like a dusting of snow.

"Oh, honey, I can handle it," he sweetly replied. "Gosh, look at this mountain of dead skin! I could make a pillow out of it. Or sell it to use in dog food!"

I laughed, my hands full of bandages, flakes of dead skin dotting my clothes like magic fairy dust. David was always joking.

Life got a monotonous kind of busy quickly. Therapy, bath, dressing, dinner. Therapy, bath, dressing, dinner. Therapy, bath, dressing, dinner. I started realizing the only mode I had was nurse mode. And that wasn't good.

One night, I crawled into David's bed with him. The house was quiet, the kids asleep. We didn't say a word. We just laid next to each other, our legs and bodies touching like awkward, first-time lovers. It was an emotionally powerful experience, both of us being still, close, tears falling down our cheeks. I thought back to the morning of the accident when we had made love. How I missed those moments. Being carefree and able to kiss, touch, caress without thinking about anything else. Without worrying. Without the fear of unintentionally hurting the one you love.

I know David craved more intimacy. I know he wanted his wife back. I remember him telling me at some point that when the nurses applied lotion on his skin, he had no sensation, but when I did it, it was a sensual experience. For me, however, putting on lotion wasn't an act of intimacy. Far from it, it was just another task to do. See, nurse mode.

I did want to be intimate with David, but I was scared. Nervous. I didn't know what the ramifications were of making love. I had talked to some of the nurses back in the BICU about whether or not David and I would ever be able to resume that part of our life. While they weren't sure how anatomically things would work, they seemed optimistic. Understandably, we had a lot of questions no one could answer. (For the sake of respecting the private nature of our intimate relationship, as well as our children and extended family, just think about the questions you would have, given the circumstances. We probably had the same ones.)

We didn't have the support we needed to adapt to life in the real world, particularly as a husband and wife. Burn philosophy has changed significantly in the past sixteen years. Today, there are more support groups, chat rooms, and conferences than there were when we entered the recovery phase. The Phoenix Society for Burn Survivors, for instance, the leading national nonprofit organization dedicated to empowering anyone affected by a burn injury through peer support, education, and advocacy is a huge resource that works with the ABA (American Burn Association, a network of medical personnel and first responders for burn support). We'll get into all this in the next chapter, but at the time David was going to day hospital, we were at a loss.

We kept trying to be more physically intimate.

Embracing each other, our warm bodies touching. But David being covered for the most part in bandages, his hands also clothed with compression gloves, posed quite the challenge. Not to mention sleeping in separate beds (we didn't share one until months later). Emotionally, David and I were beginning to bond again as a couple. But the physical aspect felt uncomfortable. It took some time, creativity and patience on both our parts, but eventually we were able to rekindle the intimacy in our marriage. It wasn't easy, but we did it.

I'll never forget about eight months after David's accident, we went to Dr. Smith's office back at Health South for a follow up. After the checkup, the doctor turned to me and asked, "So Carly, how are you doing?" and then in the same breath, "How is your sex life?"

Her questions triggered an emotional tsunami. I burst out crying in her office, which by the look on her face was an outburst she did not expect. After handing me a box of tissues, she rummaged loudly in her desk drawer, finally pulling out a business card. "Here," she offered. "This is the name and number of a really good family counselor. Call her. She'll do you some good."

I appreciated the intention, but didn't rush home and make an appointment. Not yet at least. I waited until things got a bit worse on the home front.

With David and I home, and together, we were seeing more and more issues with Samantha. She was at times angry, sometimes confused, other times sad. My gut said she was struggling with feeling responsible for the accident. I also believe a part of her acting out had to do with me unintentionally taking away her "role" when

David and I returned home. When we were, for the most part, full-time in the BICU, Samantha was the hen of the house. She understood Nathan's toddler speak and could communicate his needs to my father. She even stepped in for her grandfather and would reprimand Nathan on occasion. Once David and I were home and present, however, that unique family dynamic changed. Taking care of the house was now my job. And every now and then, I had to gently remind Samantha of that fact.

Nathan, on the other hand, occasionally showed evidence of defiance. When I'd do housework and call out for him, he'd dart toward me, yell "See ya!", and run the opposite direction. Sometimes, in the midst of playing with his toys, he'd randomly dash over to where David would be sitting in a wheelchair, smack his father in the back of the head, and run away. I struggled with wanting to discipline Nathan, but also was being tempted to give him slack considering how David and I hadn't been around the past few months.

I so desperately wanted support at the time, but not necessarily that of a professional holding a pen and paper and watching me clutch a box of tissues while I purged my feelings. I longed for peer support, another human being who had gone through similar things and had experienced the shift in family dynamics. But for now, at least, David and I were on our own, piloting our own way through this uncharted jungle, on a wing and a prayer.

In the meantime, I was nursing a quiet anger, one that bubbled under the surface. I was angry because of the accident, obviously. While we didn't know what exactly went wrong to cause the explosion, the fact remained that something did. And likely, someone was behind that something.

As time passed and we as a family got out of the house more, we ventured out to the community's Heritage Festival. There I saw a guy that worked on the construction team present when David was hurt. The smells of sausage bread and fried mushrooms invaded the air and Gerald, from our church, shouted his sales pitch in a booming voice for passersby to stop by for a free sample. I carted David around in a wheelchair, Samantha and Nathan beckoning us to the games they wanted to play and rides they wanted to ride. This man walked past us, oblivious to our presence. He held a cooing baby in his arms and walked closely to his smiling wife who adoringly clasped his hand. Not a care in the world.

Just looking at him bred a volcanic fury of anger. I hadn't a clue whether or not he had anything to do with the accident; he was just a face I could throw some blame toward. The anger subsided, not quite on that afternoon excursion to the carnival but eventually. You can't live life chained by rage; it makes forward movement impossible. Holding on to bitterness would have ruined me. And I needed to accept our current situation as a family and make peace with the fact that the accident had happened, period, regardless if someone was at fault or not. And with counseling and a ton of prayer, I did.

David

Being home was overwhelming. I couldn't stand up on my own, couldn't walk without a walker or the custom-designed bed sheet belt, and for the most part hung out in a wheelchair. I could feed myself some, but it took forever. Carly had to button my shirts, zip my pants, put my socks on, even help me while I did my business in the bathroom. The list could go on for miles.

I was dependent on Carly, who was probably the best person to be dependent on because I loved her and she loved me and she was just incredible throughout this entire process and to this day. But as a man struggling with a loss of independence, it's painful. Very emasculating. Sometimes even humiliating. I mean, having my wife wipe me after a bowel movement? Not a pretty picture. And not a scene where you want to be the star.

Whenever I thought about the accident, my injuries, the limitations, the restrictions, I retreated to a place of shadows. Questions were plenty. *How will I work again? Will I be able to even hold down a job? How will I provide for my family? What can I do to not be such a burden on them*? I tried not to focus on these issues, but they'd smack me in the face with a jarring reality whenever Carly and I would drive back and forth to the day hospital, whenever I watched her turn my alarm clock on and off for me, whenever leaning on a walker, I'd wave goodbye to Samantha as she rushed out the door for school, whenever I'd watch Nathan make a ship or aircraft out of Legos.

I had to come to terms with the fact that Carly and I were creating a new life, one that had a lot of unanswered questions we hoped to figure out as we crawled along this unpaved path at a cautious pace. I remember one day, a year or so after the accident, seeing Nathan pause in the hallway of our home and stare at the family pictures that lined the wall. He noticed me looking at him and pointed to a photo of me before the accident.

"Daddy, look. That's my old Daddy." He quickly pointed to another picture nearby of me leaving the BICU. "And that's my new Daddy," he exclaimed with a smile. Nathan's simple statements were poignant, probably the most adequate description of my recovery phase early on. Accepting a new normal. Trying to blend some of the old with the new. It took some time, but I started realizing I could find ways to contribute to my family and to society. I could learn new ways of doing things to lessen the load Carly was carrying. I was an engineer for Pete's sake. It was my job to be creative and find solutions for problematic situations. I was trained for this.

But first, there was this matter of getting out in public, one of the first ways to adjust to the new.

* * *

As Carly, Rie, and I made our way up and down the aisles of Sam's Club, the bulk product mega warehouse, I couldn't help but feel insecure. The burn injuries were visible on my face, as was the Jobst garment under my T-shirt. Not to mention, I was also walking around with a bed sheet tied around my waist, the ends held by Carly. Talk about embarrassing.

I kept my head down, trying to be inconspicuous. I didn't want to look at anyone. I didn't want anyone to look at me. If people stared at me like a freak show, I wouldn't have known it. All I could tell you about Sam's Club that day was that the floors were pretty dusty and one of the wheels on the cart my mother-in-law steered rattled obnoxiously.

I maintained seclusion in my private bubble when we headed next to Olive Garden, the Italian restaurant. Carly's dad, Chuck was meeting us there with the kids to celebrate Samantha's ninth birthday. Although her birthday was last August, this was the first time we were out in public as a family and could celebrate at a restaurant of her choosing. A belated birthday party is better late than never, right? While I had walked on my own in Sam's Club, I was exhausted by the time we got to the restaurant and used a wheelchair.

I noticed Samantha was on full alert, sizing up the expression on every single person that passed us. I know what she was wondering. Would people stare at my dad? Would they gasp? Would they point fingers and laugh? I think we were all on edge, waiting for something to happen. Waiting for someone to blurt out something stupid or stare with horrific looks on their faces. I didn't look around or allow myself to think too much. Instead, I focused on my family. I engaged Carly, Chuck, Rie, and the kids in idle chitchat, discussing possible appetizer options and the upcoming thunderstorm.

By the time the waiter brought our desserts, Samantha's topped with an array of colorful candles, we busted out in a very unharmonious "Happy Birthday" graciously joined by fellow diners.

And guess what? Our outing proved to be uneventful. No stares. No laughs. No gasps. As least according to our daughter. As Carly signed the check and we started getting ready to leave the restaurant, Samantha piped up, "Mom, nobody was mean to Dad. People even smiled at him! The waiter was really nice and people even helped us open the door or move out of our way!" A smile was plastered on her face, a beacon of light, a sigh of relief.

I smiled, too. "See Samantha," I said in a reassuring tone. "Going out with me isn't bad at all!"

"I know Daddy!" she exclaimed, getting up from her seat and taking the napkin off my lap.

As we made our way out of the restaurant, I finally looked up to see the scene around me. What caught my eye wasn't the Italian décor or laughing patrons. It was a man staring right at me. I immediately looked away, resting my eyes on the floor but something prompted me to look up again. The same man was still staring. I started feeling self-conscious.

It took a good second or two to figure out I had been looking into a mirror. This seemingly silly moment made me chuckle. I realized then that being in public, being vulnerable having my physical scars on display, wasn't such a big deal. Clothed with insecurity, I was making more of an issue out of the whole thing. I was the problem, not passing strangers. What a milestone! That day boosted my confidence and gave me the push I needed to continue my integration with society without feeling so timid and uptight.

I can do this, I thought that night as Carly helped me into my hospital bed.

She was thinking the same thing. "David," she sighed, covering me with a light blanket. "I think we should consider sending Dad back to Minnesota. I think we can do this on our own."

I nodded, thoughtful. "Yeah, it's probably time." Life certainly wasn't easy, but Carly and I were adapting to a new way of life. Oh, we had plenty of issues to work on as a family, dealing with the psychological aftermath of the accident, but we both wanted a bigger taste of independence.

"Yeah, Carly," I repeated before closing my eyes. "It's time."

10

Carly

I sat at the kitchen table, ready to jump out of my own skin. I could hear the aides in the bathroom down the hallway, both helping David with his shower. When laughter erupted, echoing throughout the house, I figured my husband must have made some kind of joke. I appreciated the health care professionals and the work they did, but I felt any personal space I had before the accident was evaporating. Well, at this point it seemed totally gone.

As I pretended to rummage through skyscraping piles of mail, bills, colorful envelopes that no doubt contained more "Get Well" cards and other hopeful sentiments, my blood continued to boil. I wasn't mad at the aide or nurse for being here. I needed them. Oh sure, by this point I could have probably helped David with his showers on my own, but I was tired of playing nurse, and still struggling to find my place as a wife.

It was the end of March, seven months after David got injured, and he was finally out of day hospital and attending outpatient rehab five days a week from 1:30-4:30 p.m. Recently, David had to go back to Galveston for about a week to get his knee patched. As his skin continued to heal, the back of his knee had split open from the constant bending in therapy.

It was a strange experience, being back in the BICU and having to relive our time there. I had begged doctors and nurses to move us to another unit, but for some reason, no one thought it appropriate to stick David in the maternity or pediatric ward. The graft, skin taken from his back, took well.

Back in Nederland, our routine resumed. Our days were full, even with less rehab time, and quickly proved exhausting. I scoured through my journals as I was writing this book, some of the experience re-reading the account was cathartic, other times it was gut-wrenching to relive. In one of my entries, I wrote down what a typical day was like at the time. As my eyes poured over those words, I felt a rush of emotion. No wonder I felt on the verge of a nervous breakdown at the time.

6:15 a.m.	*Wake up, wash my face, try to get ready, Nathan wakes.*
7:00 a.m.	*Samantha wakes, feed kids, I finish getting ready.*
7:45 a.m.	*Take Samantha to school*
8:00 a.m.	*Wake David up, take off his mask, wash his face, help him urinate, rub on lotion, put on his glasses, socks, shoes, pants, shirt. Get out wheelchair and*

	cushion. Help him out of bed and into chair.
8:30 a.m.	Get David breakfast, finish getting Nathan ready for school.
9:00 a.m.	Nurses arrive
9:15 a.m.	Take Nathan to school
10:45 a.m.	David done with bathing
11:00 a.m.	Start preparing lunch, eat
1:00 p.m.	Leave for outpatient rehab
1:30 p.m.	David therapy begins
2:00 p.m.	Me back home, put Nathan down for a nap if he is not in school
3:15 p.m.	Samantha comes home
4:00 p.m.	Leave to pick up David from rehab
4:30 p.m.	David done with therapy
5:00 p.m.	Back home, help David get situated, start dinner
6:30 p.m.	Dinner, go for walk or bike ride with family
9:00 p.m.	Bedtime for kids
10:30 p.m.	David and I asleep

Whatever "free time" I had according to this typical schedule was filled with trips to the grocery store, housecleaning, making phone calls, ordering medical supplies, scheduling and confirming David's doctor appointments, helping Samantha with homework, spending time with both kids, taking care of bills. And factor in turning every spare moment into an opportunity for David to do some at-home physical and occupational therapy. We took several walks a day around the block; I'd turn his shirts inside out so he had to turn them out the right way himself; I'd enlist his help with dinner. In other words, there was rarely a minute or two where I wasn't doing something. I had no time to soak in some white space. Catch my breath. Breathe.

At the time, David and I were on our own. David's parents, who had been pillars of support throughout this ordeal, were back in Indiana. My father, who had done an amazing job caring for our children, was back in Minnesota with my mom. And the reality check was that it was scary being on our own. We were forced to be as capable as possible, but looking back, help was monumental. Especially because I was doing everything—while running on empty. Not to mention, figuring out how to parent kids who had turned into two totally different little people since August.

I remember sitting on Samantha's bed while tucking her in one night. A scowl lined her face as she crisscrossed her arms tightly over her body.

"You guys aren't paying any attention to me," she complained, her cheerless eyes brimming with tears.

My heart broke. I had noticed that Samantha had been isolating herself, spending a lot of time alone in her room, lounging on the swing set, or playing with the cat in the yard. She seemed distracted, on edge. Whenever I'd reach out and ask her how she was doing, she'd snap back with a quick retort about being fine. Something was up. The brave front was continuing to unravel.

As Samantha turned to look out her bedroom window, a tear rolling down her face, I rubbed her arm.

"Honey, we love you so much. I know life is different now. And that since Daddy's accident, so much has changed. But we're all doing the best we can. I love you and I'm here for you. You just need to tell me what you need."

She simply nodded, still avoiding eye contact. I could

sense the fear building up in her heart.

Samantha's voice cracked with emotion as she continued, "You guys are always gone, Mom, at doctors' appointments or whatever. This is kinda ruining my life. I'm not trying to be rude, but this accident ruined everyone's life."

I listened. And with every word my daughter managed to get out, now coupled with a waterfall of tears, my heart broke a little more. What could I say to reassure her? To make things better? To relieve the crushing anxiety? To give her peace, comfort? My words didn't matter, it seemed. Samantha's feelings were what they were and I couldn't crawl into her psyche and dismantle them, as much as I wanted to. That hurt the most, that outside of telling her I loved her and being as present as possible, I was helpless.

Samantha started seeing a counselor around this time. This therapist explained that my daughter suffered from high-level anxiety in light of an unexpected accident that ripped out the safety and security she once had in life. She was dealing with an influx of emotions, always on edge, waiting for another tragedy to happen. With counseling and time, the walls around Samantha's heart came down and her old, carefree self began to emerge. While the old adage that "time heals all wounds" eventually rang true as far as her relationship with David and me, there were times within that first year I couldn't see how the brokenness could ever mend.

Nathan, too, still struggled. Because he was so young, just turning three, and not yet having developed an articulate way of communicating, he started acting out physically. He seemed angry a lot. Whenever he was frustrated, he'd sometimes break toys on purpose, bite other kids, even kick me in the shins. During his violent episodes, I'd walk him to his room and make him stay there in time-out, but he'd just use those few minutes to cause further destruction by tearing off the wallpaper border that stretched out along the middle of his walls.

Suffering from separation anxiety, Nathan hated leaving us. There were times when I'd drop him off at daycare and he'd plant his feet by the door of his class. Grabbing on to my legs for dear life, he'd cry, "Mommy, I want you forever. I don't want you to go." Can you imagine the anguish that tore through my heart? The guilt of leaving him somewhere other than home was maddening. And to stand there and gently assure him that everything would be fine as I walked into his class with him still clasped to my leg in a death grip induced such terrible feelings. There is nothing wrong with parents putting their kids in daycare, but this is not how I envisioned raising my son. Daycare wasn't something we had planned on for Nathan. But now, it was a necessity. In this season of our lives, there was no feasible way I could care for him while tending to David and everything else I had to do during the day. There wasn't enough time. And there wasn't enough me. Finally, it wasn't fair to Nathan to be dragged to every doctor and therapy appointment. He needed to play, and be a kid.

All these new changes and shifting dynamics unsettled me. I was overly emotional, crying at the drop of a hat, feeling so stressed my chest would tighten and I'd feel on the verge of hyperventilating. Staying strong and positive— what I'd done for so long—seemed eons away, a different galaxy, a different me. I'm not a therapist but I'm pretty confident those first few months I was on autopilot, fueled by the adrenaline brought on by shock. And with so many people surrounding us in support, from family and friends to community members, it was easier to be optimistic.

But now, staring reality in the face, buried in the trenches, I felt empty. Walled in by a dark place. Depleted on all fronts, spiritually, physically, sexually, emotionally, and physically. One night I gave myself a fifteen-minute break, thinking some time away from the house would help regulate my spirit. I took deep, deliberate breaths while my sneakers pounded on the pavement, one after another. I passed by a father and his son, both outfitted in leather baseball gloves, playing catch. I passed a couple on their porch, sipping on tall glasses of sweet tea. I passed by an older gentleman, doing some gardening as the last of the sunlight was disappearing under the horizon. Unfamiliar lives. Not our lives.

As I ventured back home, opening the front door to our house, I was greeted by utter chaos. The kids were upset, screaming at the top of their lungs. Nathan was throwing his video game controller at Samantha, who tried to block the object by hitting it back in his court with a video game. David was in the midst of telling them to, "Cool it. Everyone just cool it!" But his attempts at intercepting the madness were futile. No one listened. Neither Samantha nor Nathan even glanced in his direction while engaged in World War 3.

Well, I guess I won't be taking a break anytime soon, I muttered to myself as I lunged toward Nathan to cease and desist and held an arm out to Samantha to keep her from smacking her brother. I wrote this in my journal during that time.

"Oh what I would give to have our lives back—to just

rewind the last seven months and try to forget them. Every day I have reminders—a song, a memory, a photo, etc. that serves as an instant replay of the day of the accident. Sometimes I wish I could just forget. Locked my bedroom door two nights ago for 15 minutes. Was able to wash my face, remove fingernail polish and clean my jewelry all by myself—with no one asking for me, tugging at me...I want to start feeling happy again—truly happy. Not just happy for others and smiling."

My outlook improved over time, with multiple counseling sessions as a family, with David, and individually. Eventually I'd be diagnosed with clinical depression and given anti-depressants. More positive emotional changes were spurred onward once I attended the World Burn Congress and met fellow burn survivors and loved ones. I had finally found a community whose members knew exactly what we were going through."

David

I sat in the wheelchair at the table, finagling a ham sandwich between my maimed hands. Mealtimes always took forever. While it was easier—and saved time—for Carly to feed me, I had to do it myself. I didn't want to add one more thing for her to do for me on what was fast becoming a growing list.

I chewed my bites slowly, savoring real, non-hospital food, when Nathan slid into the kitchen, speeding down the floor in his socks and coming within an inch of slamming into a kitchen cabinet. He knew I was there, but didn't say a word or even look my way. Although he had warmed up to me some since seeing me for the first time in the BICU, sometimes I wondered if he ever healed from the trauma of that first rendezvous, inches away from a man he didn't even recognize. I'd often think of the time prior to the accident, when Nathan and I were inseparable. He was my little buddy. We'd play, roughhouse, toss around a ball. Now his actions consisted of not much more than a mumbled "good morning" or "good night"—and that, thanks to the faithful prodding of my wife. All my boy wants is his mom, nothing to do with me.

Samantha was quiet around me. A part of me felt she was resentful of this new life, an unexpected and unplanned new way of being that made me the center of our universe. She was also withdrawn and sometimes, like her brother, haunted by separation anxiety, afraid that leaving Carly and me would prompt another tragedy. It seemed the fire didn't just butcher my body; it also destroyed my kid's sense of security.

I remember some time in the spring I wanted to go to the movies by myself. Carly would have to drop me off and pick me up, of course, but I wanted something to do that didn't require constant care or watching or doing for me. I did have to think ahead on how I'd perform the money/ticket transaction because my fine motor skills weren't so sharp (flashback to the nightmare I had while in the traction device and trying to pay for a Coke with hands stuck in hay rakes).

My wife and I were discussing all this, she at first not totally on board with enthusiasm, but agreed that it might be good for me to do something on my own. Samantha, overhearing the conversation in the other room, bolted into the living room, shaking her head.

"No, no, no! Daddy can't go by himself. What if something happens and he needs help? What if there are mean people there? What if there's a fire?" The questions came in a machine gun succession.

Carly took Samantha on her lap and said, "Honey, Daddy will be fine. There is no need to worry. This is just something he needs to do—."

"Yes, Sam," I interjected. "I promise, I'll be fine."

Our daughter wasn't convinced and retreated back to her room, sulking. Despite Samantha's disapproval, I had a great time viewing the number one action flick at the time. The outing proved a success, absent of any problems.

Just because I was the burn survivor didn't mean I was alone waging a war. We all were. Our new situation, being home together as a family, was far from ideal, a dirt byway of deep grooves, violently interrupting what we had hoped would be somewhat of a fluid transition.

I know while I was in the BICU, Carly read Tim Hansel's book, *You Gotta Keep Dancin'* to me, but I only remembered bits. I re-read the book on my own after I got home. Throughout the book, Tim, who suffered chronic pain his whole life, extolled the virtues of having a positive attitude. As our family began to face the challenges of integrating ourselves into a new relational normal at home and into society, we had to work hard at not complaining or moping or getting stuck in the paralyzing monotony of routine. I called this having PMS (positive mental strategies). When I mentioned the term to Carly, she cringed. "Oh David," she sighed. "For Pete's sake, we have enough PMS in this house. How about saying PMA instead? For positive mental attitude?"

I shrugged. "Maybe, but PMS has a better ring to it."

We had a laugh about it that day, but implementing our positive attitude took work. A lot of work. As months passed, and eventually years, Carly and I realized the truth of the Hebrew proverbs, "A cheerful heart is good medicine." (Proverbs 17:22, NIV). This is not to say that during the process, I didn't balk at doing therapy or get frustrated learning to type again, pecking one gnarled finger at a key at a time, or get tempted to hurl a sarcastic comment at a stranger who stared at my burns for way too long. Both Carly and I have tried to be intentional about looking for blessings in the day, cultivating gratitude on purpose.

This was a lot harder for Samantha to do, especially as we started venturing out more as a family. Though our first few outings into the public had been relatively drama-free, we weren't always so lucky going forward. Samantha had grown very protective of me. One time we were out somewhere when some twenty-something surfer-looking guy caught my eye. "Whoa, dude," he said with bulging eyes, "What happened to you?" I ignored him, but Samantha glared and got surly. I can't remember what exactly she said to this "dude," but it wasn't very nice.

"Sam, it's okay," I told her. "You don't have to defend me. I'm fine." I tried to reassure my daughter that it was okay to ignore ignorant people. And while I stand behind my statements, truth was, at the time, I didn't know how to handle awkward situations like this. So I'd do nothing. By the time summer would come, however, I'd learn better skills rather than simply tuning out.

Hope started opening its doors via the Internet. Through doing some research, I found chat rooms for burn survivors.

The first few times I'd log on, I'd just read the comments, the stories of men and women, young and old, burned in chemical explosions, motor vehicle accidents, electrical fires, fireworks mishaps. It was addicting because it was like reading my own thoughts. As weeks passed, I became more participatory, sharing a little about myself, the process of recovery, what I was feeling. I didn't purge all my emotions in this chat room, mind you, just enough to relate more, and feel part of something, a community I didn't know existed. As I sat in front of the computer, pecking letter by letter like a greedy hen, Samantha glanced at the screen in passing. Curiosity got the best of her.

"Daddy, what are you doing?" she asked.

"Oh, just chatting with some folks who have been burned just like your Daddy."

"Can I see?"

Her piqued interest opened a door to the online burn community. It gave us, and Carly as well, a forum to learn, to vent, to share, to encourage, and to remind ourselves that we Bowers were not alone. That in itself brought relief, hope, even a promise of the life, one of independence, joy, and sense of normalcy, that was possible. It was during one particular chat session that I learned about the Phoenix Society and the support and resources they had available for the burn survivor community.

At this point, my physical and functional progress had plateaued. I could walk without the walker, help out around the house, get in and out of chairs, and be more independent as far as bathroom duties were concerned. Though I was a lot more functional than I was at my admission into Health South in December, I wasn't making huge strides and found myself getting depressed at times. I needed more support, live support.

* * *

"Okay, David," my physical therapist said, holding the door to the cramped backseat space in her compact car wide open. With a nod and a sweep of her arm she motioned, "Hop in buddy."

I looked at her and smiled, trying not to seem intimidated by the claustrophobic space. "You got it!" It took a while, but I did it. I backed into the car seat, using my elbows on the car door and door jam to lower myself onto the seat cushion. Then I bent my head into the tiny car and leaned over toward the other side of the car until I could pull my legs back and in the vehicle. Not being able to fully bend my legs, it took a grand effort. After a long five or ten minutes, I grinned, a bit winded.

"Way to go, David!" my therapist exclaimed. "Now get your butt out of there and let's do it a couple more times."

I groaned loudly, doling out some faux theatrics. While getting in and out of the car wasn't necessarily fun, I knew I had to do it. After all, Carly and I had a big trip coming up. And I'd have to not just get in and out of airplanes, but taxis and subways and trolleys, too, and who knew what else? And while I was pretty adept at getting in and out of SUVs and pickup trucks, small spaces were quite the challenge. I had a lot to practice.

By the time summer rolled around, David and I decided to take a trip to San Francisco to attend the Phoenix Society's World Burn Congress, a gathering of about 350 burn survivors, medical professionals, and first responders. We were in desperate need of support and longed to be surrounded by people who could empathize with our situation. We figured we could turn this into a road trip, an adventure of sorts with the kids before dropping them off with David's parents in Indiana so David and I could attend the three and a half day conference alone.

We drove from Nederland to Dallas to spend a day with some friends (Glen and Helene and their children). From there the four of us took our sweet time and drove to Hastings, Minnesota to spend time with my parents. Then we took off to Indiana to visit with David's parents, where the kids would stay until we returned. I scheduled therapy appointments for David when we were in Minnesota and Indiana so he wouldn't fall behind. Though the entire trip took close to six weeks and we avoided the rush factor, it was a pretty tiring, but fun, journey. Our family shared many laughs and silly moments along the way. And once a day, I helped David with showering and wound care. While we were visiting with both sets of parents, each of them hosted an open house and invited family and friends to visit with us so we could acknowledge their prayers and support. What a powerful time!

Finally, David and I flew to San Francisco. Friends of Keith and Marilyn's picked us up at the airport and drove us to our hotel. David and I had some downtime before, and even at times during, the conference. So, we had planned to venture out into the beautiful city. Why would we even consider holing ourselves up in one place when San Francisco was beckoning us with inviting, open arms? I mean, really, we couldn't not explore some of this beautiful city and figure out why visitors tended to leave their hearts there. David and I enjoyed the Golden Gate City, saying "yes" to scenic rides on cable cars and a walk down the famous Fisherman's Wharf to peruse the crowded waterfront marketplaces, indulging in fish-n-chips, and catching sight of sea lions basking in the sun. Our excursions out into the busy real world were the start of a beautiful thing for both David and me. It brought out another layer of normalcy that we were desperately searching for.

The conference itself was an incredible learning and healing experience. We listened to keynote speakers share their stories and medical experts offer industry break-throughs and challenges. We also met fellow burn survivors during the breakout sessions. It was amazing to see so many people who had been severely burned now thriving in their lives. Getting together with some of these men and women and talk about the different aspects of burn care and life in general, the highs and the lows, was monumental. I felt wrapped by a sense of belonging.

I'll never forget meeting a woman named Sue Lugli from California. She and her husband had been burned in a motor home accident. After the last meeting of each day, we chatted away for hours. She was the first wife I had ever met who understood my situation. And well past the recovery stage, Sue had plenty of wisdom and life experience to pass down, which I hungrily devoured. We are friends to this day.

I remember another particular moment, one that wasn't so great. I sat in one particular breakout session, listening to a panel of men and women, some of whom had been married at the time of their injuries, some who had recently entered the dating scene. At the time, it felt like every single person on the panel was whole, emotionally and mentally. When the moderator asked the panel, "Were there any issues as far as physical intimacy?" I burst out crying— like mascara-ruining-swollen-eyelids-ugly-crying. Nobody was forthcoming with any real issues they faced, whether depression, or intimacy struggles with their spouse, or feeling bitter. All I could think was, "Oh my gosh. David and I are so messed up." That day I vowed if David and I were ever in a position to share our story, we would be transparent and real.

The Phoenix Society teaches about the importance of taking care of the caregiver. I heard someone speak on this topic at the World Burn Congress meeting we attended. While the idea certainly caught my attention, the idea didn't quite sink in. Taking time for me seemed foreign, silly even. I assumed life would fall apart if I took a break. It also seemed selfish.

Sometime after this conference, David coordinated for me to go to Dallas for a weekend, to get away and visit with my good friend Helene. I was resistant at first, but I went. Helene pampered me silly, gifting me with massages and cooking delicious meals, hoping to get my mind off everything at home. As it turned out, the break was refreshing. I can't say I was fully sold on the concept of self-care, but I started to see its potential. Being with my friend without the weight of endless responsibilities lightened my spirit. But while the time was refreshing, it didn't make me forget or take away the realities back home. I've learned since then, to take more time for myself. Self-care makes me a better wife, mom, and friend.

David

One of the things that stuck with me during this conference was one of the speakers offering how important it was to look people in the eyes, not just while speaking to them in conversation, but even in passing, on the street, in a restaurant, in a mall. My mind journeyed back to my first trip out in public, strolling down the aisles of Sam's Club with my head down and doing the same during dinner at the Olive Garden. I could barely look up, let alone look strangers in the eye. The speaker had said, "Roughly ninety percent of the population isn't staring at you. They are busy. Busy in their life and busy in their own worlds. Still, it's important to engage others and that's why eye contact is vital. It keeps you connected, a part of the community, even if others don't understand your world."

Later that weekend, Carly and I took a break and headed out of the hotel to do some shopping and sightseeing. I had no interest in rifling through knickknacks in local shops, so I told Carly, while pointing to a nearby empty bench, "You go on ahead. I'll just wait for you over here." I planted myself down on the wooden seat and she kissed me goodbye on the forehead. For the first time since the accident, I started people watching. Wearing a wide-brimmed hat and my JOBST body garment, I watched men in suits hurrying by, construction workers on their lunch breaks eating sandwiches out of paper bags, tourists brandishing huge cameras around their necks mapping out their next destination, groups of young women carrying shopping bags and chatting with one another.

The speaker was right, I thought. *Nobody is paying any attention to me. Everyone is busy doing their own thing. I'm just another face in the crowd.* I gained confidence that day, simply by opening my eyes to and staring into the world while sitting on an uncomfortable bench. And as I waited for Carly to return, I smiled, breathing in the warm air, feeling every bit free.

The speakers at the World Burn Congress also taught me to "know my story." Sounds obvious, right? For me it wasn't. The fact is, even though the majority of people are busy, distracted by their own selves and their own worlds, there are folks who will stare or ask sometimes dumb, sometimes legitimately curious questions about your injuries. Depending on the circumstance or genuineness of the person asking, I learned to have a short story ("I was burned at work and I'm doing fine now."), the longer version, and a sarcastic one ("I was eaten alive by a Chihuahua," or one of my all-time favorites, "I have leprosy."). Some people will have more of a sincere interest than others, perhaps because they know someone with similar injuries, as opposed to the nosy folks who are curious about the weird looking man.

I also learned—and this was incredibly helpful—that I had to stop comparing what I couldn't do post-accident to what I could do pre-accident. Every time I found myself getting discouraged by my perceived lack of progress or inability to type like a fiend or not being able to pump gas for my wife, I had to remember my lowest point—lying in an emergency room and having a zero chance of survival. It's about perspective. Focusing on what you can do makes life easier. It's like what Leonardo DaVinci said, "Shadow is the obstruction of light. Shadows appear to me to be of supreme importance in perspective, because, without them opaque and solid bodies will be ill defined; that which is contained within their outlines and their boundaries themselves will be ill-understood unless they are shown against a background of a different tone from themselves."[16]

The Phoenix Society and this particular World Burn Congress made such an impact on Carly and me that we made the decision to start giving back. Like any opportunity to serve others in any capacity, it helped us focus on others rather than ourselves. After attending that first conference, we connected with Carolyn Barfield, one of our former nurses from Health South that we became friends with whose husband and son were burned in separate incidents. Together we started up a support group in Beaumont, Texas for burn survivors. Carly and I also started volunteering for the Phoenix Society, helping out at future events and sitting on planning committees. By the third or fourth year, Carly and I were speaking on topics including family care, taking care of caregivers, intimacy after a burn, and long-term aftercare. Samantha even talked one year at a breakout session about being a child of a burn survivor. Many years later, at our prompting, the Phoenix Society implemented a charter program specifically designed for kids and we volunteered our services.

Carly

On the way home from the World Burn Congress, knowing the first anniversary of the accident was coming up, David and I decided to throw a party to celebrate his life. We didn't want the day to be a somber reminder of exactly what had transpired a year earlier. We invited family members and folks from church, Praxair, the community, and all the medical and healthcare professionals who were a part of David's journey for the past twelve months. We simply wanted to provide a meal and say thank you for everyone who prayed and helped us in any way. So, yes, it was indeed a celebration, specifically a BBQ, which seemed a fitting theme.

My dear husband partnered with Big Nate from youth group to write a poem for the party.

Ode to an Ear

It all started off as a fine, fine day,
But it ended up in a place far away
Swinging with Nate and breakfast with Sam,
Grilled quesadillas for lunch and then a quick bam.
In the flash of fire,
I looked like a tire.
Friends and family started a prayer,
They flew me to Galveston for the best of care.
The surgeries began to replace my skin.
They placed it on me very, very thin.
My head was shaved to get what skin that they could
But when I wasn't looking, snip, snip, my ear was gone for

> *good...*
> *They hung me from the ceiling*
> *So my skin could do its best healing*
> *My skin got thicker,*
> *But in November I got sicker...*
> *As I was sick I had a bad fever*
> *Those darn youth group kids were watching 'Leave It To*
> *Beaver.'*
> *I had to relearn how to walk and stand,*
> *All through this the church got a bigger band.*
> *It has been a long recovery for this past year,*
> *With all things considered, it is not too bad to live without*
> *an ear.*

David then copied these poetic words on a huge poster board and placed it on a table at the entrance of our house. Alongside this giant poem sat an enlarged photo of David's ear prior to the accident, as well as a Barbie-sized wooden coffin covered in black tulle and cradling a plastic ear. Morbid, right? What a way to welcome incoming guests!

About a hundred people showed up for the party, including the ER doctor who had first examined David at St. Mary's, some EMT folks, including the paramedic Jay, and a couple of therapists and nurses from Health South. Balloons and streamers, once again, flooded our yard. Music blared over loudspeakers. While guests sipped on cups of ice-cold lemonade, Clyde grilled burgers and hotdogs. Co-workers from the plant made ice cream out of liquid nitrogen. And before the afternoon was over, we served a giant sheet cake complete with flames and, of course, an ear courtesy of red and orange icing.

The celebration was such a hit, we've had one every year since, complete with themes, coordinating décor, and for the first few years my dad's artistic talents rewriting famous songs (including "The Monster Mash" and "Staying Alive") with new lyrics about David. We also included in our celebrations opportunities for attendees to reach out to the burn community. We've asked folks to donate care package items (toiletries, prepaid phone cards, snacks, water bottles and the like), which our family boxed and mailed to several burn units across the country. Now we only accept monetary donations for scholarships to send burn survivors to the World Burn Congress. What a feeling to give back, however little we can.

David began reconstruction surgery at this time. His hands were a priority because they were badly damaged and not very functional. However, we didn't know the extent of the damage until that first elective surgery, which was performed back at UTMB in Galveston by a plastic surgeon. It was worse than we thought. The joints, tendons and ligaments that held David's fingers in place were severely impaired. During the procedure, doctors cleaned out his joints as good as they could, as well as peeled all the skin off the backside of his fingers and sewed his right hand into a surgically cut pocket in his groin. This procedure was called a flap. The theory was that the relatively unburned skin on his groin would be more flexible and the fat would allow the tendons that had scarred down to the bone to move again. It was a complicated surgery and lasted almost seven hours. And David's hand was kept sewn into his body for close to six weeks. Three more surgeries were required to take his hand out of his body and separate the fingers.

The surgeries went well, but didn't create any miracles, as the existing damage was pretty bad.

Around this time, we'd had too many scheduling issues with the home health aides who were coming by daily to help bathe David and help with wound care, so we opted to tackle these tasks ourselves. Even with his limited hand function, David had figured out how to do most of the shower-related tasks and I concentrated my efforts on his skin dressings.

David

I admit. When I started reconstructive surgery, I had grand notions that my mangled hands were going to be fixed. After all, since the accident doctors and nurses kept telling me that "everything was going to be okay," which I thought meant that things would get back to what they had been before the accident. That my fingers would work, and I'd easily be able to pry open a can of soda or button my shirts. The truth, as told by the plastic surgeon post-operation was devastating. My existing damage was far worse than he had expected and though future surgeries would be an option, my hands would never be as functional as he had hoped.

On the way home from an appointment with the plastic surgeon, Carly and I stopped at a beach after driving off the ferry. Still sitting in the truck, we stared out over the horizon. Gentle waves lapped at the shore, glimmering like diamonds in the setting sun. Both of us were in tears. I mourned the loss of my hands. It was time to bury the dreams of having pre-accident hands for good. I had to trade that expectation with concentrating on learning new ways of doing things. This was a long journey, which continues to this day.

11.

For the joy of the Lord is your strength.

Nehemiah 8:10, NIV

David

I stood in line behind ten people, all of whom wore annoyed expressions much like the DMV employees who sat in front of them behind glass partitions.

"Next!" someone behind the counter blared with a hint of an attitude.

The last time I heard that word was about ten minutes ago. *I'm gonna be here forever*, I thought. But I didn't mind. Really, I didn't. I was simply excited. I was renewing my driver's license, which had expired while I was in the hospital. Having Carly drive me around everywhere was getting old. I felt like a kid relying on mommy to get to the mall. After I outfitted our truck with a steering knob on the steering wheel, giving my right hand better range of motion and control, as well as a button to start the car, I practiced driving around the block and in a parking lot. But I wanted to legally drive further than a few hundred feet. So I was not at all bothered by however long I had to stay in the musty, floor-to-ceiling beige-colored building plastered with glossy posters reminding visitors not to drink and drive.

"Next!" *Was it my turn already?*

Based on prior DMV experiences, I assumed the employee who would help me would be cranky, impatient, and roll her eyes in response to my questions. I couldn't have been more wrong. The second this lady took one look at me, she smiled and very sweetly said, "How can I help you sir?"

As it turned out, she had a relative who had been severely burned and therefore showed a great deal of compassion during our entire interaction. While the renewal process didn't demand a road test, just a slew of identification paperwork, I wanted to get behind the wheel and be given an official thumbs-up before I was legally allowed on the road. You know, just to be safe.

Two or three hours later, having passed the road test, I walked out of the DMV parading my newly laminated driver's license like the proud parent of a newborn. While I couldn't twist off the cap of the gas tank to fill 'er up, I could drive.

A lot of changes were underway, even on the home front. On the road to being, as I liked to say back then, non-functionally independent, I thought about going back to work. Clyde had been trying to convince me for months to go back to work at Praxair, that they'd find a place for me somewhere, but as anxious as I was to restart my career, the thought of working at the plant was troublesome. And the more I thought about it, the louder my "no" resounded. It just wasn't realistic. I was regaining function, but doing even the most basic things took me ten times as long as the average person. After some soul searching, prayer, and lots of discussion, I decided to take disability retirement from Praxair.

While Carly and I were ping-ponging our thoughts about going back to the company, one of us broached the topic of moving, an equally frightening and exciting notion.

Carly

David and I had talked about relocating our family since our first anniversary party. It was a tug of war, not between us, but in each of our hearts. Nederland was our home, a place where the community—our church, our neighborhood, our friends, folks from Praxair—galvanized in support of our family. They came alongside us and welcomed us back into their lives after we returned home from the hospital. They helped us move forward and get back to living. And yet, it was a place where so many memories simmered and reminded us of how our life had changed in drastic ways.

David and I wanted a fresh start. We were beginning to get acclimated to our new life and what better way to continue the adventure in a place where no one knew your name? We also realized how important it was to have family nearby. They had done an incredible job pitching in when we needed help. It takes a village to do many things, not just raise a child.

After months of researching, talking with friends, family members, and even strangers in the different places we were interested in, we settled on moving to Ladoga, Indiana. A small town full of charm and hospitality, it flaunted wide-open spaces, very unlike the suburban community where we lived in Texas. Ladoga was only an hour away from David's parents and ten hours from mine.

Before we moved to Indiana, David met with Dr. Herndon, the director of burn services at UTMB, who recommended a burn surgeon, Dr. Joe Mlakar (Dr. Joe), in Fort Wayne, Indiana. Though we didn't immediately make the three-hour drive from our new home to see Dr. Mlakar, we did about a year later when David needed a patch graft. A caring, funny, and personable man, he was quite the refreshing change from some of the arrogant physicians who had recently treated David.

Leaving Nederland in February of 2002 was a tear fest. Much of the support network we had grown over the past few years showed up during the week before we loaded our belongings into the back of a semi-trailer truck. David, the kids, and I hugged, cried, and voiced our appreciation to each person who had been there for us through our darkest moments. I'll never forget crossing the Indiana state line, much of our home in tow. Flurries cascaded lazily down, officially welcoming us into a much cooler and snowy winter climate.

Our family started digging into life again. Nathan started a preschool he loved and quickly made new friends. Samantha, too, liked her new sixth-grade class, and especially the fact that David and I signed up to be room parents. The four of us plugged into a local church, and I volunteered to help on the children's ministry team. The change was good, challenging at times, but it seemed life was beginning to settle down.

David

Life slowed down in Indiana. No whirlwind of doctor or therapy appointments. No influx of visitors or home health aides. Our days revolved around our family. And it was good. Real good. Until the questions started coming.

In moving to a small town like Ladoga, after the boxes are unpacked and you figure out the best butcher shop, the cheapest gas station, the closest convenience store and the public school rhythms, everyone is going to know not just your name, but also your story. Or ask questions. And unlike Nederland, where much of the community we interacted with knew I had been burned in an explosion, no one in our new hometown had a clue of our backstory. So at the grocery store, the bakery, school functions, and Wal-Mart, people would introduce themselves and I would follow suit, not revealing much other than my short story. This I could deal with. What got tough was hearing over and over the question, "So David, what do you do?"

In hearing those words, my jaw would clench, muscles tighten. I wasn't offended at the question; I just didn't know what to say. It made me uncomfortable but the feeling had nothing to do with anyone but me. I was struggling with my identity. I had been a successful engineer for ten plus years and now, considering my limitations, I was technically retired and disabled.

Retired.

It took a while to get used to saying that word. I didn't quite know how being retired fit in to who I was, or who I used to be. Saying the word made me feel depressed, even emasculated. But the more I was asked and the more I answered the same, the idea began to register. Being retired stopped feeling like evidence of my loss but mere fact. I began to learn that who I was as a person had less to do with just my engineering degree, my established work history, and my accomplishments. My identity is grounded in Christ and what's most important is my relationship with Him and my family.

Another challenge that surfaced, in light of being retired and having an open schedule, was the abundance of time to think. Though early on in the BICU, I had started to struggle with the "why" question, after the move to Indiana, the introspection grew full-fledged. I was grateful to have Carly by my side and together we began to excavate the jagged landscape of questions, asking ourselves things like:

Was God personally involved in orchestrating the accident?
Was He punishing me for doing something wrong?
Didn't God love us?
Did He have the power to stop the accident?
Did He even want to prevent it?
What good could possibly come out of this?

My wife and I talked into the wee hours of many a morning, digging through our feelings and thoughts not just surrounding the purpose of the accident—if there was, in fact, one—but searching out the character of God. Because the more questions we had, the more we realized the answers had to do with who He is.

Over the course of time, I concluded that God wasn't a hard-hearted and ruthless being who delighted in punishing us peons down below for whatever purpose.

I couldn't imagine a God I loved, a God who I served,

saying on the day of my birth something like, "One day, I'm going to cause David Bowers to be at the wrong place at the wrong time and be engulfed in an oxygen fire that, though will not take his life, will make it a living hell. And I'm going to do this so he can help others down the road." No, that's not the kind of God I believe in. God doesn't purposely compose awful tragedies in our lives, yours or mine, so one day we can start up a support group or pray with more empathy had we not suffered.

"God does not cause evil and God does not cause suffering. But He does allow them because they have a purpose. God permits them and then He uses them. God is an expert at bringing good out of bad."[17] This quote from Rick Warren makes me think about the many burn survivors I have met over the years and how encouraged I've been by their strength, their resolve, and their determination to live well. Their stories have impacted me for the good and I hope in some way I can do the same for others.

I've since come to terms that some questions are unanswerable in the present life. It's like the Apostle Paul wrote, "For now we see only a reflection as in a mirror; then we shall see face to face. Now I know in part; then I shall know fully, even as I am fully known." (1 Corinthians 13:12, NIV)

In 2004, our family spent a week at the Wind River Ranch in breathtaking Estes Park, Colorado, where we continued to visit each summer for the next few years. A Christian dude ranch, it provided us with a time of spiritual refreshment, a space to be still in a scenic backdrop of majestic mountain views, tranquil ponds, and wildlife. We, along with a number of other families, spent time riding horses, learning how to square dance, hiking, river rafting, as well as participating in group devotionals, set praise and worship times, and teaching from Pastor Jeff Warren from Texas.

That week, Pastor Jeff focused on the biblical story of Job, a righteous man who endured unspeakable tragedy, losing his health, his property, his wealth, and his children. Though I had heard the story many times before, listening to it in the breathtaking setting of the great outdoors had a profound impact on me. While millions of stars blanketed the night sky and a majestic 14,000-foot mountain range loomed in the backdrop, Pastor Jeff spoke about God's greatness, His might, His authority, and His power. Sitting on a rocking chair next to my wife, I felt small. And I finally came to terms with letting the "why" question go. I realized, in such a deep and personal way, that God is much bigger than me. His ways are not my ways. And who am I to question day after day why He does or does not do certain things? He is all-knowing and all-powerful. I am not. Carly is not. You are not. Only God is.

I may never know the reason for the accident, and that's okay. Though, as I've said earlier, asking questions is a natural wiring of the human mind and God can handle them. The more you focus on the "why," the more you get stuck and the deeper the root of bitterness grows. I remember in one of our conversations Carly telling me, "Instead of asking God 'why us?' I think I'm leaning more toward 'why not us?'"

And why not us, indeed.

Carly

In 2005, our entire family attended the World Burn Congress in Baltimore, Maryland. While networking with other attendees at the kickoff event, a man wearing a blue shirt came over and tapped me on the shoulder.

"Excuse me," he said, looking at David and me intently. "Were you guys at the hospital in Fort Wayne a few months ago?"

As I thought the question over a second, my husband sidled up to me and answered the guy, "Yeah, we were. We had to go to the clinic for a follow up appointment after my surgery."

The stranger nodded and looked relieved. "Yeah, I thought so." He bit his lip and took a breath while David and I waited for him to continue. Turning to David, the man said, "Our son was in the ICU at the time, having suffered serious burns. I'll never forget watching you bee-bopping your way into the office wearing shorts and a T-shirt. You and your wife were chatting and laughing, just carrying on without a care in the world. I couldn't take my eyes off of you guys." Tears brimmed his eyes as he lowered his gaze slightly. "I had no idea what my son's life would or could be like. You guys gave me so much hope."

David and I were overwhelmed at his outpouring of gratitude, for nothing in particular that we did. Meeting this gentleman was proof that in ways seen and unseen, we can all make a difference in someone else's life—and never even realize it.

* * *

Life became semi-normal at this point. David had a few more surgeries, including one to patch up a graft on his right shin, a few to release contractures on his neck, eyelids, and armpits, and a few more on his right hand. There was one surgery in particular in which he almost lost his hand. This scare prompted a long conversation between my husband and me. We talked about the risks of surgery versus possible gains and decided taking another chance of completely losing his hand was not worth the possibility of gaining another two degrees of motion. David took control of his surgical future then, focusing on ones that posed few risks and were critical, like patching up grafts he would tear. And he made sure to schedule them when they were convenient for him and our family.

In the spring of 2006, Samantha had a show choir competition in Indianapolis, which is an hour away from Ladoga, the same day Nathan had a local basketball game. After dropping off our daughter at her school where she'd be bused to the venue, we watched Nathan play ball. When the final buzzer sounded and cheers rang out for the winning team, the three of us got in our car and drove to Indy for Samantha's competition. David's parents, Marilyn and Keith, were waiting for us there to cheer on their granddaughter.

On the drive, I noticed David was quiet, not saying much in reply to my chatterbox self. He also looked pale, grey even.

Sweat started to form around his forehead when he looked at me and said, "Carly, I don't feel so good. I think I'm coming down with something."

"Do you want to go home?" I asked, concerned.

David shook his head. "No, I want to see Samantha sing," he insisted, pooh-poohing his symptoms as the onset of a probable flu virus. Almost halfway into the concert, my husband looked horrible, his face sweaty, skin cold and clammy. And his right leg hurt so bad, the slightest movement made him wince. Right after Samantha and her choir's performance, Keith drove David and Nathan home, while Marilyn and I waited for the competition to end. Before it was over, I phoned home to check on David.

"He's got a 102 fever," Keith informed me. "Chills and everything. It's definitely the flu."

When morning came, we suspected the flu was not the culprit. David's leg was bright red, hot to the touch, and swollen so badly, his sock wouldn't even fit over his ankle. We called Dr. Joe who practically commanded us to drive immediately to the hospital in Fort Wayne. There David was diagnosed with cellulitis, a serious bacterial infection which, if caught on time, is treatable, with high doses of antibiotics. If the infection festers, however, as it did in David's case, it can cause sepsis, blood poisoning, and can be fatal. My husband had to stay in the hospital for a week, receiving intravenous antibiotics to treat both the cellulitis and resulting sepsis.

The cellulitis started recurring regularly, once every few months. And every time he had a flare up, we were thrown into a tizzy. Surely, this wasn't normal and posed a serious risk to David. What if one time the sepsis moved in rapidly and we were too late? What if the antibiotics didn't work? What if I end up losing David?

We started asking around, exploring options so his body would be better protected from these recurring infections.

Someone had recommended wearing compression stockings with silver fiber in it; silver contains antimicrobial properties and therefore acts as a guard against infections. It worked. David was cellulitis free for eighteen months. Then, it started happening again. We realized the infection would sometimes occur before we had a trip planned and he was running around preparing for it. A hard man to slow down, David's body had a long way to catch up with his high level of internal energy. We had to come to terms that this side effect of the burns is likely to be long-term. We always keep a bottle of antibiotics close by so he can be treated immediately wherever we are.

Life moved on relatively medical drama free for a few years. In September of 2013, we were proud and honored to celebrate the wedding of our daughter to Rudy, whom we love. What an amazing day, especially in light of the fact that fourteen years earlier, we didn't know if David would survive long enough to see this day come. God is so good!

David

Cellulitis wasn't the only complication I dealt with, though between my outbreaks and the beginning of 2013, I had no medical problems other than an annoying sore on my right shin the size of a pencil eraser. By summer it had grown to the size of a quarter. Because the sore was getting bigger, Dr. Joe treated it for a ton of wacky infections. Also, a dermatologist had performed a punch biopsy to check for potential skin disorders, but results came back clear. I figured the sore was just an annoying complication from all the infections.

In the spring of 2014, Carly was asked to speak at the American Burn Association's 45th Annual Meeting in Boston, Massachusetts. As "luck" would have it, while she sat in on a meeting I ran into Dr. Sanford, one of the burn specialists who had initially treated me at UTMB in Galveston and now worked at the Loyola University Medical Center in Chicago. It's amazing how God works to put people in the right place at just the right time. We don't believe in coincidences at all.

We shared a heartwarming reunion in the hotel lobby when the topic turned to my current medical condition. I mentioned something in passing about the ongoing sore when Dr. Sanford's expression turned grim.

"You need to be careful about squamous cell cancer," he said.

Hearing him mention the C-word was such a shock, I almost dropped the folder of burn resources and booklets I was holding from the last session.

"The problem might have to do with the cultured skin, although we aren't completely sure," Dr. Sanford continued. "Back in 1998, before I started treating you, I had a patient, a teenager, who had similar skin grafts and he ended up dying of skin cancer about a year ago. There's only a few people in the world who have had this type of cultured skin, so it's hard to get statistics, but I wonder if the cancer and the grafts are somehow linked."

I nodded, giving myself some time to let his words sink in. Cancer?

"Now, David. I don't want you to worry. And I'm certainly not saying you're going to get cancer. I just want to warn you, just something to keep in the back of your head, especially if that sore doesn't heal."

"Um, okay," I voiced, thoughtful, but not overly concerned. Frankly, I was confident I did not have cancer. The recent biopsy I'd had came back clear so though Dr. Sanford's words were startling, I simply filed away the warning. I met up with Carly later that evening and told her about the conversation. I didn't want her to worry, so I kept the news nonchalant. Not that my calm tone worked.

"Cancer?" Carly blurted, eyes wide in shock. "Cancer?!"

"Honey, we already had a biopsy done. It was negative. I'm good. Everything is fine."

"But, no—" she stammered. "I want more information. You can't just drop the C-word and expect me not to worry!"

I wrapped my arms around her and in a very reassuring voice repeated, "Everything is fine, Carly. Trust me. I don't have cancer."

The sore never healed. And it got bigger. It had grown to the size of a coaster, 2"x 3." I experimented with different medications, none of which worked. I also underwent non-surgical methods, including patching the area with a synthetic material which didn't take. Finally, June 19, 2014, I was scheduled for surgery with Dr. Joe to have the open wound cleaned, debrided, and covered with healthy tissue.

Right before being wheeled into surgery, I told Dr. Joe, "One of my previous doctors at UTMB told me to watch out for squamous cell cancer, in light of the cultured skin grafts. Would you biopsy the area to check?"

He looked doubtful. "David, there's really no need. Skin cancer does not present itself with the kind of sore you have. In my professional opinion, a biopsy is quite unnecessary."

Not willing to drop the issue I asked, "Well, can you do it anyway, Dr. Joe? Just for giggles?"

"Of course," he agreed, chuckling. "But trust me, it's not going to be cancer." His smile and overall confident attitude was reassuring.

A week later, Carly and I sat in his waiting room for a post-operative appointment. As we flipped through magazines much about nothing, the door to the waiting room opened. It wasn't a nurse telling us to come on in; it was Dr. Joe. "I'm ready for you, David." Carly and I looked at each other, fear drawn in our eyes. He'd never before personally came to get us in the waiting area. My wife clasped my hand tight and together, led by our doctor, we walked into a procedure room.

I sat on the table, nervous, as Dr. Joe took off the dressings to look at my skin. Quiet, forgoing the small talk, he began his spiel. "I'm happy to report your graft looks great." Then, the dreaded pause. "But I'm afraid to tell you the pathology report from the biopsy revealed cancer. Frankly, I never imagined that's what would show up."

Carly and I looked at him, stunned into silence as he continued. "I could remove the cancer, but depending on how deep it is into the leg, I may or may not be able to close the wound up again. If the cancer has made its way into the bone, amputation is a strong possibility."

I looked at Carly. She didn't even bother to temper the tears that were rapidly falling down her face. We left the office that day, shocked, crying, not making a set plan of what to do. The three-hour drive back home was quiet. As I was doped up on painkillers, my wife drove, wiping away the constant stream of tears. Samantha and Nathan and our parents were texting and calling, leaving voicemails, but we never responded to any message, paralyzed by shock. We also wanted to share the news in person first with our children.

I know burns. I know all about burns—skin grafts, common infections, bedsores, scar tissue—all these things. But cancer? Didn't know a thing about it. So I spent the drive researching, scrolling up and down WebMD and Googling our options, worse case scenarios, how bad the diagnosis really was. I don't remember every piece of material I read, but the prognosis wasn't hopeful. I ended my search feeling discouraged, questioning my mortality.

When we arrived home, we told our children. Nathan was recovering from leg surgery and Samantha and her husband, Rudy, were caring for him at the house that day. Nathan, just like his dad, was calm and collected. He gave us hugs and said with confidence to his father, "You'll be okay." Samantha, like her mom, was an emotional mess. She cried, which fueled more of my tears. Heaviness filled the air that evening. But we took the opportunity to lean in toward one another, and pray. It was pretty amazing to deal with this crisis alongside our older children, not needing to protect them from the hard stuff. Later that night we also told our parents who, though devastated at the shocking news, gave us their full support and prayers.

On Sunday, two days after the initial diagnosis, Carly reached out to Dr. Sanford via email for help. We didn't know whom else to turn to. "Come to Loyola on Wednesday," he emailed back late that night.

The three-hour drive to Chicago on July 2nd was tense, at least at first. A few minutes before we left home, Carly had sent out a note on Facebook telling our friends what we were dealing with and asking them to blitz us with Scripture. Only a few miles out of town, the first "ding" of replies to the post sounded.

Carly read aloud the first response. "Fear not, for I am with you. I am your God. I will strengthen you. I will help you. I will uphold you with my righteous hand" (Isaiah 41:10 NIV). My heavy heart began to lighten.

Then, another ding. "Be strong and courageous," another friend encouraged. "Do not be afraid; do not be discouraged for the Lord your God will be with you wherever you go" (Joshua 1:9 NIV).

The dings never stopped the entire way. Together, Carly and I fought our fears with faith. Though the angst of pressing into more unknown territory lingered, the more Scripture we read out loud, taking turns driving, the more God's truth submerged our anxiety, the foreboding, into deep waters. The fear was there but faint, without power to destroy our spirits.

By the time we saw Dr. Sanford, he had spoken to a good friend of his who also happened to be an oncologist, as well as the medical team at UTMB. For the next several hours, I had a number of x-rays, MRIs, full body scans, CAT scans, bone scans, basically the radiological works.

Ironically, this was the same day as our 20th wedding anniversary. To celebrate, after the myriad of tests were over, I took Carly out to dinner at a Polish restaurant. I was hypnotically drawn to this hole in the wall eatery because of its vintage neon signage. The restaurant featured the most delicious pierogis I'd ever tasted as well as décor that hadn't been updated since the 1970s. Quite a memorable venue for an anniversary dinner.

Wielding his influence, Dr. Sanford was able to get most of the results quickly. The good news was that the cancer hadn't spread to other parts of my body. The bad news was that surgery was the only option to determine how deep the disease had infected the leg. More grim news followed, repeating Dr. Joe's earlier sentiments.

"I hate to have to say this, David," Dr. Sanford warned. "But you might be looking at a potential amputation, depending on whether or not I find cancer in the bone." We arranged surgery for the following Thursday.

Life felt big again, too big. Overwhelming. Confusing. I thought for sure I had a lifetime ahead of me, filled with monumental occasions like cuddling my newborn grand-children one day or helping Nathan fill out his college applications. I was emotional, yes, but I also felt at peace. Should I get thrown a sucker punch by a worse case scenario, I'd had a good life. I married the love of my life. Watched my beautiful children grow up. Enjoyed the love and support of loved ones all around. Carly had asked sometime before the surgery if I wanted to write letters to anyone. Goodbye letters. Not only did I offer final words with pen and paper to my wife, my kids, my parents, and my in-laws, I also wrote down instructions to my pastors about my funeral. Seems morbid, but I was grateful for the opportunity to be able to put words on paper and leave this written legacy to the ones I loved. I filed away those letters, just in case.

Since that dreaded conversation with Dr. Sanford, I had a

perpetual knot in the pit of my stomach, a headache that never seemed to go completely away, a spot in my chest aching from fear and worry, and tears, sometimes sobs, that came uncontrollably as the weight of what we might be facing smacked me head on.

Sometimes my mind would try to stabilize the runaway thoughts saying repeatedly, "It's just skin cancer." But I knew better. Most people who get a skin cancer diagnosis don't undergo tests for brain, liver, lungs and bones and the doctors don't have them contemplate the prognosis of an amputation of a limb. David and I were walking in dangerous territory and we understood that.

It was a struggle to stay positive and for my thoughts to not drift off to the scary, dark places. I turned to prayer and reading God's word, remembering His truth. As we anxiously awaited the trip back to Loyola for David's surgery, we felt God's loving arms wrap us in His care through others. Friends brought us meals and even helped with yard work. We received cards in the mail and thoughtful notes on our Facebook page and emails, all letting us know we were not alone in this battle.

Samantha, Nathan, David, and I drove to Chicago the night before David's scheduled surgery. As per surgery rules, he couldn't eat past midnight, so we indulged ourselves at a steakhouse, David eating enough for two days. The four of us spent the night at a nearby hotel, using our private family life to gain spiritual strength and believe for miracles. Together we prayed for David and lifted each other up with Scripture.

Taking the drive to the hospital for the surgery, my thoughts ran rampant and fear tried to creep back in.

Though I was scared, I stood firm, resting in the assurances of God. When life spins out of control, we're sometimes only left hanging on to our faith. It's in these moments, when faith is all we have, that it becomes much more evident how important it really is.

Right before we pulled into the hospital parking lot, I turned to David in the car and said with confidence, "This is not how our story ends, you know."

"You're right," he nodded, reaching for my hand over the console. And with a wink he said, "We can't have a bitter ending, not after going through all we've been through. And hey, regardless of the outcome, we still have to remember that God works all things for the good of those who love Him. God's got this, Carly," he voiced with confidence. "God's got this!"

"I know He does," I said, reinforcing David's assurances. "Besides, I'm already having trouble writing all the chapters to our book. I don't need to add any more!"

"That's right!" Samantha and Nathan piped up from the back, poking their heads through the space between the two front seats.

While I accompanied David to prep for surgery, Samantha and Nathan stayed behind in the waiting room. Only two people at a time were allowed in the surgical unit and I wasn't going to chose between my daughter and my son. After an hour, I joined my kids. I was delighted to see Marilyn, Keith, Amber, and Teresa in the waiting room. They had just driven in from Indiana to support us and buffer us in person with more prayer. For the next few hours, the seven of us encouraged each other, grounding ourselves in faith as we waited for Dr. Sanford to tell us David's surgical outcome.

Then, the news. Wearing scrubs and a cap, Dr. Sanford walked into the waiting room with a smile. "Guys, I have good news. We removed all the cancerous tissue, about a 5"x 9" section of David's leg, including part of his bone. And though we have to wait for the pathology reports to come back to confirm he's cancer free, I can tell you that we got clear margins."

Praise God! Some of us cried, others whispered prayers of gratitude. We were elated, and able to breathe a little bit easier and deeper.

"David's going to need a few hours to recover, but then you guys can see him," Dr. Sanford said, before giving me a bear hug and leaving the room.

Tears of joy filled the waiting room as we hugged one another and thanked our heavenly Father for the news. We took a break and headed down to Johnny's Beef, a legendary local joint that serves the world's best Italian beef and brought back a monstrous sandwich and lemon ice for David. Prior to the surgery, he playfully demanded I bring back the famous roast beef sandwich.

Only two people at a time were allowed to visit patients in the BICU, so my kids, in-laws, and I took turns spending time with David, watching him savor the juicy and mouth-watering beef and revel in the good news.

Not wanting to stay in the BICU overnight, Dr. Sanford had given us permission to spend the night at a local hotel once David's pain was under control. So after chowing down his Johnny's beef, David and I made a break for the non-hospital accommodations while the rest of our crew drove to our home in Ladoga.

The nurse who wheeled David out toward our car said, "Boy, you sure didn't stay here very long."

My husband grinned. "We don't like to stay in hospitals. Too many sick people."

We saw Dr. Sanford a week later. As he anticipated, the pathology reports confirmed there were no remaining signs of cancer and that it hadn't spread to other organs. He did advise, however, that because this type of cancer spreads to the brain, liver, and bones David would need to see a dermatologist and oncologist every six months to watch for other spots, just in case. Though optimistic he warned, "David's body is covered in millions of these cultured cells that originally were grown quickly in a lab and then told to just stop growing. Some of these cells might go haywire. This sore may have been the first evidence and chances are likely they'll be others. Time will tell."

As of the time of this writing, every six-month check up has been clear. And we continue to pray and believe in God for a cancer free future.

David

I love the scene in *Shawshank Redemption* when Andy (played by Tim Robbins) sits with fellow prisoner Red (Morgan Freeman) in the exercise yard, contemplating life after prison. Andy allows his imagination to run wild and dreams of a life in Mexico. As the two friends talk more, Red admits he's doubtful he would make it on the outside; he's been behind bars for so long. Before the scene ends with Andy walking away, he offers Red a profound statement, "It comes down to a simple choice, get busy living or get busy dying." That's exactly what I've learned to do—make the choice to get back in the game. To turn my back on a life of misery and find joy.

It's been sixteen years since the accident. I'm alive. I'm well. And as of today, still cancer free. On an emotional front, I suffered from Post Traumatic Stress Disorder, PTSD, as a result of the accident. While I didn't experience severe disabling symptoms, certain things trigger the memory of the accident and cause me to break out into night sweats. If I watch a movie or see anything explosion-related (like a rocket launch or being at a Japanese hibachi restaurant and watching the chef arrange onions in a fire-shooting volcano), I get startled and immediately close my eyes. Later that night, I'll wake up drenched in sweat. While these incidences have lessened, I still experience them every now and then.

Though I need to take breaks and not run myself ragged, I'm physically active and, dare I say, in pretty good shape. Out of the thousand things I could do before I got hurt, I can still do nine hundred of them. So I don't stew and dwell on the lost hundred. They're just gone.

I've not only learned to walk, I've climbed mountains. On one of our annual trips to the Wind River Ranch, I hiked Estes Cone, a 6.4-mile trail along the Rocky Mountains, which offers an 11,000-foot summit. Though I'd hiked other mountain trails before in the area on other visits, this was the first time I made it to the top. A soft breeze surrounded me as I climbed the strenuous path, taking time to catch my breath. As I paused, I deeply inhaled the fresh mountain air and scent of the pine forest, and soaked up the scenic landscape that surrounded me. And then I scaled back up the rocky ridge.

By the time I reached the summit of the cone shaped mountain, between the high altitude and the rigorous climb, my heart was beating out of my chest. Barely able to breathe, I sat down and wondered how I'd make it back down the mountain safely. While the path was worn, marked by the steps of travelers before me, the descent was steep and dangerous, a mix of sand, gravel, and slippery rocks that moved at a touch. And being physically exhausted didn't help matters. Still sitting, I pulled out my pocket Bible and began to read Psalm 121 [NIV] aloud.

> *I lift up my eyes to the mountains—*
> *where does my help come from?*
> *My help comes from the Lord,*
> *the Maker of heaven and earth.*
> *He will not let your foot slip—*
> *he who watches over you will not slumber;*
> *indeed, he who watches over Israel*
> *will neither slumber nor sleep.*
> *The Lord watches over you—*
> *the Lord is your shade at your right hand;*
> *the sun will not harm you by day,*
> *nor the moon by night.*
> *The Lord will keep you from all harm—*
> *he will watch over your life;*
> *the Lord will watch over your coming and going*
> *both now and forevermore.*

As I read aloud the Psalmist's prayer, the Spirit of God

began to envelop me, breathing into my body and soul, strength, power, might. I called Carly and together we read it again and prayed. It was a beautiful moment, a holy one of reflection and gratitude. Then slowly and carefully, using a slow and careful pace, I trekked down the rugged path.

It was quite an accomplishment. Only a few years earlier doctors weren't certain whether or not I'd ever walk again. I can do many more things than walk or climb mountains. I shovel snow. I mow the yard. I landscape. It may take several attempts and some extra time to do things that require fine motor skills, like using a knife, pliers, or a hammer, but I can get them done. I open soda cans by using the end of a spoon to gain leverage, pick up small objects like coins off the ground with a sheet of paper, and use pliers to hold a nail so I can pound it in with a hammer.

While my burn injuries have not stopped me from living and enjoying life, there are precautions I need to take. Since my body cannot regulate temperature and I can easily succumb to heat stroke, it's important for me to stay hydrated at all times. On a recent mission trip abroad, as I sat on a train, I started sweating profusely. Luckily, I was able to quickly take cover in an air-conditioned café at the next stop and gulp down some water. On another recent mission trip, I started overheating in a venue without air conditioning, I discovered a creative way to cool down—lying down on a concrete floor near a vent. Whatever works! I also need to wear sunscreen all the time and moisturize my skin regularly. Though my skin is healed, it's very sensitive. If I bump my legs against a hard object, it will likely produce an open spot.

Despite the many things I'm capable of doing and the

independence that I have established so far, my range of motion is still limited. I have a tough time reaching things on the top shelf of the grocery store or bending my legs in small and tight spaces like a compact car. And sometimes it's tough to get a good grip on things; I've been known to drop some plates while washing dishes. And I sometimes have a difficult time with touch-activated devices, like ATMs or airport kiosks.

There are a few good things about not having the best of functioning hands. One, not having fingerprints, I have a great opportunity to begin a life of crime. Two, I always win at Rock-Paper-Scissors.

Carly

The first few anniversaries of David's accident were extremely emotionally difficult. I would dread the upcoming date on the calendar. I'd map out the hour hand on the clock and remember what I was doing that day like it was yesterday. By year twelve, I remember driving down a street in town and seeing a banner across a bridge that listed the date August 20. I was taken by surprise. It was the first time that day I remembered what day it really was.

Back in 1999, many people would tell me that the flashbacks would ease up, the nightmares would cease, the go-overs in my head would subside. I thought these well-intentioned people were nuts. But turns out, they were right. Today, rather than submerge myself in the awful memories of that day and that time, I am grateful. I am so thankful God spared David's life and healed him. Words cannot even begin to express the amount of gratitude I feel.

We have wept bitterly. We have felt discouraged and broken. We have prayed with every ounce of strength we could find. But with God's help, and the support of an amazing family and wonderful friends, we have grown in our faith individually and as a family. We have laughed. We have found new purpose. We have found hope. And we have found joy.

It would have been easy for us to get stuck in the tragedy of the accident, the losses we have experienced along the way. We have deliberately chosen joy and hope in our lives day to day. Yes, some moments are better than others. And there are always highs and lows. But through it all, God is faithful. Helen Keller said, "The world is full of suffering. It is also full of the overcoming of it."[18]

It's easy to tell someone not to give up, especially to those who just lost a child, or have been given a few months to live, or have struggled for years with depression, or have lost everything they have worked so hard to build. But the fact remains that giving up, abandoning all hope, will only guarantee your place in continued darkness. If you are going through a difficult time right now, I want to encourage you. Trust God even if He seems silent and the circumstances before you look bleak. Forgo pride and lean on others who are willing to act as pillars, praying for you, and blessing you with their time, their love, and their support. Immerse your mind and your soul in God's Word "for they are life to those who find them and health to one's whole body." (Proverbs 4:22, NIV)

Miracles come in different shapes and forms. Healing may come through spirit and not flesh. God's idea of tomorrow may be painted with different colors than you would have liked. But He is still God. He is still good. And He is still faithful. I don't know what our future holds, but I know Who is holding it. And to me, to our family, that's more than enough to know.

David

Pain is an unavoidable part of life. Aeschylus, the Greek playwright, wrote, "Who, except the gods, can live time through forever without any pain?" I'm sure you have experienced suffering of some kind, whether death of a loved one, abandonment of a parent or spouse, addiction, trauma, disease, or bankruptcy. Though we cannot escape pain, we can learn to live with it. Through such painful difficulties, we learn who we really are and, better yet, who we can become. Pain can either destroy us or shape us.

I'll never forget when Nathan was around nine years old, he asked me as I tucked him into bed, "Dad, if you could go back and not have your accident, would you?" At first, I wondered if the question was a stall tactic to gain a few extra minutes before lights out, but knowing my son and his bend toward philosophical questions, I entertained the powerful inquiry.

I paused for a moment before replying, "Nate, there are times I wish that I would have had gloves on so I'd have more hand function today, but I honestly don't wish the accident away. Our life has been incredible because of what has happened."

I meant every word. I truly believe the accident has made

me, and our entire family, who we are today. Our faith has grown. We're able to show more empathy to others who may be different than the norm. And we have a firm perspective on the stuff that really matters.

I used to question the future, the landscape, the possibilities, the challenges. But tomorrow doesn't concern me much anymore. I've learned, through fire of the body and struggles of the soul, that God goes before me. And He will always prepare my way.

Acknowledgments

This hasn't been an easy book to write. For years, David and I have been hesitant to share about what our family has been through on such a public level, simply because we're more behind-the-scenes kind of people. We don't like to be in the spotlight. When we've been asked to share in the past, we have done so but we have never gone out looking for speaking opportunities to tell the story. For years, we've hidden behind the cloak of humility, because we were fearful that pride would creep into our hearts if we shared a story that was just about us. On many occasions, over the years, we've been nudged to write this story but we always made excuses as to why we weren't cut out for that job. With the gentle and persistent prompting of many friends, family members, and speakers we finally recognized that this was something that God was asking us to do. We were pushed out of our comfort zones and were reminded that sharing our experience didn't have to only be about us; it could be used as an opportunity to give God the glory He deserves.

So, with much prayer and consideration, we chose to be obedient and we took a leap of faith as we relied on God for help, wisdom, and the determination to share what He has done in our lives.

While our journey does involve tragedy, this is not the theme of our lives. Through darkness, shadows, and many unknowns, we have found victory and hope. This is our message. Healing has been an ongoing process, but through it all we have grown closer to God and to each other. Even in our bleakest moments, we've been blessed with reminders that God has a plan, a purpose, and a hope for our pain.

To God. We pray this honors You and brings You the glory that You alone deserve. Thank You for giving us a reason to hope and the opportunity to find joy, even in the hard times.

To Our Children, Samantha & Nathan. You've had to learn how to deal with life's mountains and valleys at far too early of an age. Sacrifices have been made, as you've had to deal with doctor's appointments, hospital stays, pesky, unwanted infections, and a cancer diagnosis. You've developed a different perspective on life simply because life didn't always look "normal." We're blessed to see how you've both grown into compassionate, caring adults who see beauty in all people. We're sorry that we couldn't protect you from all of the pain, but we're grateful for how we've learned to walk together, side by side, as a family, through this crazy journey called life.

To Our Parents, (Keith & Marilyn and Chuck & Rie) and Our Siblings, (Teresa & Randy and Amber & John) for the selfless, sacrificial, unconditional love you've showered us with over the years and for never hesitating to dive into whatever needed to be done. Because we have had to walk through tragedy together, we truly believe that our relationships have grown stronger through the years. Thank you for your generous compassion, your kind words of encouragement, your tender-hearted nurturing, your support and understanding when you've been near to us or many miles away. We've depended on you for numerous things and we couldn't have done this without all of you!

Sometimes we are blessed with special types of friendships that last a lifetime and span the distance of many miles. This has been especially true with *Gordon Gathright, Jackie Philyaw, Rob & Melissa Kleber and Helene Millsap. Gordon*, you've been our spiritual advisor, mentor and friend for over 20 years. We're so blessed that you were a part of bringing the two of us together. Thanks for those late night phone calls, for Gopher runs, and for the prayer coverage you've always provided. *Jackie,* (a.k.a. "Oscar") You were our partner in crime while we were in youth ministry together and braved the lizard infestation of the youth room with Carly. Thanks for generously being with us through the tears and laughter and for loving us so well. *Rob & Melissa*, thank you for a friendship that always seems to pick up where it left off, no matter how long we've been apart. Rob, thanks for making sure Carly was taken care of those first few days after the accident. You made sure she got fresh air, sleep and food each day. Melissa, thanks for getting David to the church on time all those years ago and for acting as our very own personal medical specialist while David was hospitalized. Thanks for educating us on creatinine levels and for allowing Rob to be in Texas. Your friendship has truly stood the test of time. *Helene*, we became instant friends when we first set foot in the Proverbs Sunday School Class and even though miles have separated us, our friendship never dwindled. Thank you for being at the hospital, for just simply listening to Carly when she'd call and for pampering Carly with a Girl's Getaway weekend so she could escape the craziness of life for a few days. Your faith and friendship have been a lifeline.

To the First Responders in Mid County, specifically *the Groves Fire Department, the Paramedics and EMT's of Rural Metro Ambulance and the doctors and nurses at St. Mary's Emergency Room. Jay St. John,* you were made to do this job and you do it so very well. Thank you for taking such good care of David at such a critical time. Your ongoing friendship is truly a gift.

To the Doctors, Nurses and Therapists at UTMB Burn Unit in Galveston, Texas including *Dr. Sanford, Dr. Herndon, nurse Rachel, nurse Verna, nurse Jamie and Sheila.* Thank you for not only meeting the physical needs of your burn patients, but for realizing our entire family needed emotional and spiritual healing as well.

To the Doctors, nurses and Therapists at HealthSouth in Beaumont, Texas especially *nurse Carolyn* who always went beyond the call of duty and who helped us remember to laugh again.

To TIRR Therapy in Mid County, Wishard Hospital in Indianapolis, St Joseph's BICU in Fort Wayne, and Loyola Hospital in Chicago, especially *Dr. Sanford.* Thanks for investing in our family again after all these years. We feel like our reunion was not by accident.

To Plastic Surgery Innovations, specifically *Dr. Joe and Darlene.* You always saw the person behind the scars and treated us with dignity and respect. Thank you.

To The Phoenix Society for Burn Survivors. Carly remembers calling your office out of desperation, needing support for our family and our unique struggles. Instantly, she felt a connection that cannot be explained. Your dedication to the burn community has enabled us to get our lives back. We've been amazed at all you have accomplished over the past sixteen years in the lives of so many. Thank you for providing us with the necessary tools, for creating a community and for addressing the specific needs of families and children impacted by burn injuries.

To Clyde Howard. You are an outstanding example of what a true servant leader is. We appreciate the fact that you were always much more than a boss—you are a friend. Thank you for taking such good care of our family from the moment we set foot on Texas soil and the days that followed. You've always gone above and beyond the call of duty.

To the Guys at the Groves, Texas Praxair Plant. Who knew that 7 guys could accomplish so much, have so much fun together, or grow into such a tight-knit family while working? Thanks for initially welcoming our family to Southeast Texas and for supporting our family in big and small ways. We appreciate that you continued to include David in the activities of the plant, even after he was unable to return to work.

To the Praxair Company. Thank you for looking out for our family before and after David's accident. You took such good care of us while David was in the hospital. Thank you for minimizing the financial stress, for donating blood, for visiting with us, for notes of encouragement and for making David feel like he was still part of your team.

To Don McIntyre and the staff at Wind River Ranch. Ya'll provide so much more than a fun family vacation spot. By ministering to us, you've provided our family with a mountaintop experience. Wind River provides a safe, majestic backdrop to sort out life's bigger issues. Over the years, you've modeled what a heart of a servant looks like and you've pushed us to be more like the hands and feet of Christ.

To the Speakers at Wind River Ranch, including Jeff Warren, Pike Wisner and Susie & Will Davis Jr. Your thoughtful and provoking teaching at the Ranch was what allowed us to move beyond asking "Why?" and to recognize that God is God and I am not. Your teachings also made us begin to wrestle with the idea of needing to share this story with others. We recognized that by hiding behind our curtain of humility, we might have been robbing God of the glory he deserved. Thanks for pushing us out of the boat and for believing in us.

To Our Prayer Warriors at Wesley United Methodist Church in Nederland, Texas, the church that *Sparkles*. You welcomed our family into your midst when we moved into your community, you supported us while David was in the hospital and more importantly, you accepted us and helped us find our new roles after David's accident when everything had changed and we were learning to make the transition from victims to survivors. *To Gerald Nelson* who encouraged us early on to write this story. We wish he was still here to read it. To *Marilyn Myers* who understood the power of prayer and used emails to connect people across the globe. Without her DBU's this story would have been almost impossible to write, because we were able to piece some of the details together by looking back at these daily updates she provided. *To The Proverb's Adult Sunday School Class.* Your friendships mean the world to us. You carried our family by lifting us up in prayer and by ultimately being the body of Christ to us. *To The Parents of the Youth Program at Wesley UMC.* We are honored and amazed that you trusted us to lead and love your kiddos while we were at Wesley. *To The Kids of the Wesley UMC Youth Groups*, who are now all grown up. Words cannot even begin to describe the place you hold in our hearts. You each are a true blessing to our family. Thank you for all the adventures, laughter and learning we experienced together. Remember to never pass by a rotten watermelon or bowling ball on the side of the road. We love you!

To The people of Montgomery County, Indiana. You welcomed us into your community with opened arms and in doing so, you provided us with the fresh start our family needed. Thank you for not being afraid of a family that looked and acted a little different.

To Our Friends and Pastors at Rock Point Church in Crawfordsville, Indiana, specifically *Pastor Brian Saunders* for mentoring us and for nudging us out of our comfort zone. You challenged us to start sharing what God's done in our lives more with others. *To Pastor Terry Thompson* for teaching Truth and not being afraid to tackle our tough questions. *To Our Former & Current Small Group Bible Study Members.*

By stepping up into a role of leadership, our faith was tested and stretched. By diving into God's Word together on a regular basis, our faith and our friendships have grown. We're honored to have been the group facilitators on occasion and equally blessed by the opportunity to just be a participant at times.

To Carly's Jesus Girls & Jesus Girls 2. Thank you for the accountability you've provided Carly, for not being afraid to dive into God's Word, for your encouragement and for covering this project in prayer from the beginning to the completion.

To AJ Gregory, Esther Fedorkevich and the entire Fedd Agency. We appreciate that you took an interest in this story and told us we needed to share it with others. It wouldn't have been possible without the countless hours you each put into this project. I'm not sure you knew what you were getting yourselves into when you took this project on, but we are forever grateful that you did!

To the countless people who have come alongside our family throughout the years in big and small ways—they were all big to us. You prayed, brought meals, sent cards and notes of encouragement, watched our children, spent time with David, helped us with yard work, visited us in the hospitals, gave blood, helped with household chores, gave us books that inspired and gave us a sense of hope, assisted with homework, listened to us cry, shared in our laughter, pushed and persuaded us to try new things. You have served alongside us and helped with some of our crazy ideas. You have loved on, taken care of and supported us in so many ways. The list is far too long to mention you all by name, but please know that your selfless acts of love never went unnoticed. We are grateful for each and every one of you. We deeply apologize if we have inadvertently failed to mention anyone.

To The Reader. Thank you so much for picking up this book. Please share it with someone else. We are honored to have the opportunity to encourage others who are facing hardship. It is our prayer that through this story and this book you will see the light and love of God shining through and that you will find hope, even when you can barely see where the next step in life will lead. Thank you for your interest in this story. Our hope is that you don't read this book and think it's just a story about our family—it's so much more than that! This is a powerful story about what God has done for our family and a gentle reminder of what He can do for you as well.

~Carly & David

NOTES

(Endnotes)

1. Joan Didion, *The Year of Magical Thinking* (New York: Alfred A. Knopf, 2005), p 3.

2. Ralph Waldo Emerson, *The Conduct of Life* (Boston and New York: Houghton, Mifflin, and Company, 1904), p 313.

3. Hugh Prather, *Notes to Myself: My Struggle to Become a Person* (New York: Bantam; 20 Anv Rep edition, 1983), p 24.

4. Jack Canfield, Mark Victor Hansen, *Chicken Soup for the Soul: Teens Talk Tough Times* (Connecticut: Chicken Soup for the Soul Publishing, 2009) p 31.

5. Elie Wiesel, *From the Kingdom of Memory* (New York: Schocken Books, 1990) p 249.

6. C.S. Lewis, *The Business of Heaven* (C.S. Lewis Pte Ltd, 1984) p 242 .

7.. Tim Hansel, *You Gotta Keep Dancing* (Colorado Springs: Cook Communication Ministries, 1985) p 48.

8. Ibid p 55.

9. Morris C. Katzoff, *A Bit at a Time* (Indianpolis: Wordclay, 2008) p 135.

10. Joyce Meyer, *Living Beyond your Feelings* (New York: FaithWords, 2011) p 12.

11. Emily Dickinson, Thomas H. Johnson, *The Complete Poems of Emily Dickinson* (New York: Back Bay Books,

1976) p 116.

12. Charles Dickens and George Cruikshank, *Works of Charles Dickens* (London: Chapman and Hall, 1866).

13. Dan Millman, *Way of the Peaceful Warrior: A Book that Changes Lives* (Tiburon, California: H J Kramer, Inc., 1984) p 113.

14. Joni Erickson Tada, Jon & Friends Radio Broadcast, date unknown. (From *Cradle My Heart*, Kim Ketola (Grand Rapids: Kregel Publications, 2012)

15. J. Burns, *The Church of England Magazine*, Volume 1 (London: Robbson, Levey & Franklyn, 1836). https://books.google.com/books?id=-tfNAAAAMAAJ&printsec=frontcover&source=gbs_ge_summary_r&cad=0#v=onepage&q&f=false

16. Sean Cubitt, The Practice of Light (Cambridge: MIT Press, 2014 p. 171.

17. http://rickwarren.org/devotional/english/god-is-an-expert-at-bringing-good-out-of-bad

18. Helen Keller, *The World I Live in and Optimism: A Collection of Essays* (New York: Dover Publications, 2009) p 89.